A
Treasury
of
Things
to
Make

A Treasury of Things to Make

by the Editors of
SPHERE MAGAZINE

Platt & Munk, Publishers/New York

Editorial coordination: Elizabeth Rhein
Design: H. B. Smith

Library of Congress Catalog Card Number: 77-80345
ISBN: 0-8228-7720-1

Contents

Introduction

A Treasury of Things to Make is for everyone — from the skilled craftsperson who wants new inspiration to the beginner with an ambitious imagination. In its pages you'll find a wealth of ideas for creating a good-living environment with a collection of craft projects particularly appropriate for active, lively people.

Full-color photography illustrates each and every project and serves to suggest uses or settings for the finished items. Instructions containing very intricate techniques, such as basketry and paper sculpture, also have series of how-to photographs so you can see exactly how each step of the process is achieved.

Each of the nearly sixty projects also includes background information on the item or technique, suggestions for using the project as a steppingstone to others of your own design, and special helps for choosing materials and completing the project more efficiently. Wherever possible, alternative materials and methods are also suggested.

A Treasury of Things to Make is one of the most comprehensive books of craft projects ever published. Use it to explore new avenues in your favorite crafts, as an introduction to crafts you have been wanting to try, as a source for decorating and fashion ideas and as a book to own and display proudly. In these pages, you and your family will find a wealth of new and exciting ideas for creating beautiful, one-of-a-kind, personal masterpieces.

Choosing and compiling the craft projects to appear in A Treasury of Things to Make was a rewarding but difficult task, for there were hundreds of projects in the pages of SPHERE from which to select. The job was made easier, though, through the efforts of many people, some of whose names are listed here.

Caroline Kriz reviewed the final manuscript and offered valuable editorial assistance throughout the project. Barbara Ottenhoff proofread the entire book. Many of the line drawings were done by John Widmer. Elizabeth Rothman reviewed all knitting instructions.

Production was accomplished through the efforts of SPHERE staff members Dennis Balas, Michael Keating, Sheila Lange, Ron Phillips, Donald Spurlock, Deborah Webster and Patricia Witman.

A Treasury of Things to Make is above all the product of the many talented designers and photographers whose work appeared in the pages of SPHERE. Their names appear on page 224.

Joan Leonard
Editor, SPHERE

Chicago, Illinois
August 1977

How to use this book

Little or no experience is required to complete any of the projects in A Treasury of Things to Make. Special skills — including illustrated how-to's for every knitting, crochet, embroidery and needlepoint stitch used in the book — are covered in detail in the Technique Directory. You need no outside sources to use A Treasury of Things to Make; all the information you need for any project is right here.

After you've selected a project on which to work, the first thing you should do is read the Instructions through very carefully. You might decide that the project is too advanced for your skills or not one you want to do just now. This is also the time to decide whether you want to make any changes in the project as shown, and if so, to make notes on what you need to do to achieve these changes. If you wish to alter the design, for best results follow the stated method for incorporating your design.

Inventory the materials you have on hand to see exactly what you will need to purchase. Make all the necessary measurements at home and take them with you when you set out to purchase materials. The introduction to the project will tell you where the more unusual materials can be purchased. It's a good idea, especially if you are new to a particular craft, to take this book to the store as well.

The instructions for each project are broken down into two sections: "You need" and "To make." "You need" lists all the materials required for doing so in a clearly written, easy-to-follow style. When necessary or appropriate, diagrams illustrate a portion of the process.

"Optional" listings in "You need" can be either a choice between two or more items or an item that is not required to complete the project.

Some of the projects require patterns. Smaller patterns have been drawn to full size; larger patterns were placed on a grid and drawn to a size that is easy to enlarge. Instructions for enlarging and transferring patterns immediately follow the Pattern Section at the back of the book.

When you're unfamiliar with a certain stitch or technique, practice it on a scrap of the fabric or material before beginning the project. This will save time and money since it will lessen the chances of damage.

Before you start to work, assemble all the materials in one area. Prepare your work surface, if one is required. Prepare any necessary Patterns. While working, be sure to complete each step of the Instructions before going on to the next. Take your time; spending a little more time frequently results in a much finer finished piece.

For the left-handed
All instructions in this book are written for right-handed people. Where necessary, left-handed people should simply reverse the hands as well as the technique to achieve the same results. Practice on scraps before beginning work if you're in doubt on how to transpose instructions.

PROJECTS

Soft Sculpture Rabbits

These fabric rabbits are so lifelike it's hard to tell them from the real thing! But they're made from a variety of fabrics—cotton velveteen for the bodies, fake fur for the necks and tails, satin for the ears—which give them the feel as well as the look of life.

Do most of the assembly on the sewing machine. Then give the mother rabbit and her three babies individual personality and attitude by taking strategic tucks during and after construction. Take the tucks by hand where the Head meets the Side, where the Side front meets the Underside, between the Ears at the top of the head and anywhere else you desire. Follow the photograph or make your own changes in pose, expression or shape as you go; your soft sculpture will become a reflection of your own personal creativity.

The approximate finished size of the mother rabbit is 22" x 11". Each baby is about 10" x 8". Two babies are white with gray spots and one is gray with white spots. Stitch the completed rabbit family together for display or leave them separated.

INSTRUCTIONS

You need

- Soft Sculpture Patterns (pages 178-179)
- Enlarging Patterns materials (see page 206)
- Transferring Patterns materials (see page 206)
- 2 yds. 39"-wide gray cotton velveteen
- 1½ yds. 39"-wide white cotton velveteen
- ½ yd. pink satin
- ½ yd. white fake fur fabric
- Scrap of black cotton velveteen
- Scissors
- Gray and white thread
- Needle
- 2 bags polyester fiber stuffing
- Pink embroidery floss

To make

1. With Enlarging and Transferring Patterns Materials and Soft Sculpture Patterns, make pattern pieces for Mother and for Babies.

2. Cut pieces from fabric as indicated with Patterns. With dressmaker's carbon paper and tracing wheel, mark construction dots and lines on wrong side of fabric.

3. With white and gray velveteen scraps, cut spots to desired size, allowing ⅜" all around for seam allowance.

Mother Rabbit

As you stitch or when you have finished, take tucks by hand at various places to shape sculpture as desired.

1. Machine stitch Sides to Back. Machine stitch Underside to Back and Sides. Machine stitch Neck to top front end of Underside. Set aside.

2. Fold each Paw on fold line; stitch along dotted edge. Turn right side out; stuff with polyester fiber to desired firmness. Turn under open edge and hand stitch both Front and Back Paws to Underside, positioned as on Pattern; Mother Rabbit should lie on Underside.

3. Turn under seam allowance along dotted line on Tail; turn under seam allowance on Undertail. Hand stitch together with wrong sides together leaving open at Tail base, stuff lightly. Turn under open edge and hand stitch Tail to back end over seam line. Tack opposite end of Tail to Back so only fur side shows.

4. With right sides together, stitch 1 satin lining to each Ear, leaving opening at bottom. Turn right side out, baste open edge closed, fold softly along Soft Fold lines.

5. Machine stitch Head Sides to Head Top/ Back, stitching Ears in place at notches. Hand stitch Nose/Chin to Head Top. Stuff to desired firmness.

6. With threaded needle, take 3-4 stitches from Eye to Eye through Head, pinching Head at Eyes to shorten distance for needle to pass through. Pull to indent Eye area slightly. Turn under edge on Eye; hand stitch to Head over tacks leaving small opening. Stuff Eye through opening until firm; complete hand stitching.

7. With pink embroidery floss, stitch Nose Mark in place on Nose.

8. Stuff body to desired firmness. Hand stitch Head to body opening, adding stuffing when stitching is almost complete, if necessary. Turn Head at angle as you stitch to give realistic pose.

Babies

1. Construct 3 babies in same way as Mother; take tucks by hand at desired seams to shape.

2. Hand stitch spots to bodies in desired positions.

3. If desired, tack Babies to Mother.

Turkish Needlepoint Rug

One of the most valued possessions of the Turkish nomad was a lightweight pileless rug called a <u>kilim</u>. Carried everywhere, this bright piece of fabric was used to wrap goods, cover beds and, most importantly, to insulate tent dwellers from the severe cold of winter in eastern Turkey. The fabric was made of wool, mohair or other types of goat hair woven in strips on portable looms, and the strips were sewn together to complete a rug.

The design is based on one repeated pattern, but the colors vary strategically from square to square. The different hues create the illusion of continuous change; viewed from separate angles the pattern fades, only to re-emerge. In Turkey this configuration was called "designs approaching infinity."

We adapted a classic kilim for American needlepoint, using 3-ply Persian wool and 14 mesh mono canvas. The stitch, an Upright Gobelin, closely approximates the original weave. Continental and long outline stitches form accents. The Gobelin is worked in many lengths, covering from one to eleven threads of canvas.

The finished rug measures 25½" x 57".

INSTRUCTIONS

You need

- 2 yds. 40"-wide 14 mesh mono needlepoint canvas
- Masking tape
- Dressmaker's pencil
- Rug Patterns (page 180-181)
- 3-ply Persian wool yarn as follows:
    - 11 oz. warm red
    - 9 oz. brown
    - 8 oz. camel
    - 7 oz. sienna
    - 6 oz. cream
    - 5 oz. blue
    - 4 oz. putty
    - 3 oz. salmon
- Size 18 tapestry needle
- Stand-up needlepoint frame (optional)
- Steam iron
- 1¾ yds. medium-weight canvas
- Carpet thread
- Heavy-duty sharp needle

To make

1. Cut needlepoint canvas to 31½" x 63" size. Encase edges in masking tape. Mark 1 short end of canvas "top." Along top edge, with dressmaker's pencil, mark the point 7½" from top edge and 15½" from left side edge. This is the Starting Point for the first motif to be worked only (see Rug Patterns 1 and 2).

2. Beginning at Starting Point, with tapestry needle and all 3 strands of Persian yarn, work motif shown in Pat. 1 following colors listed for Square 3 in Pat. 2. Work color areas within square in alphabetical order. After completing Square 3, work Square 2 on each side, then Square 1 on each end. Work all succeeding rows in same manner, beginning with center square and working out to edges. Work all 55 squares according to Pat. 2.

3. Work border along short edges of rug as in Pat. 3. Face design in opposite direction along 2nd short edge. Work camel and brown as outlined in Pat. 3 along side (long) edges.

4. When needlepoint is complete, trim canvas to 2" wide around needlepoint along all 4 edges. Turn under to wrong side of rug along edge of needlepoint so no canvas shows on right side; with steam iron, gently steam on both sides. With tapestry needle and Persian yarn, tack folded canvas to wrong side of rug, making sure stitches do not show through to right side.

5. Cut medium-weight canvas for backing 2" larger than hemmed rug on all edges. Turn under 2" so backing matches rug, and with needle and carpet thread, stitch backing to rug along edge. ○

Knitted Baby Caftan

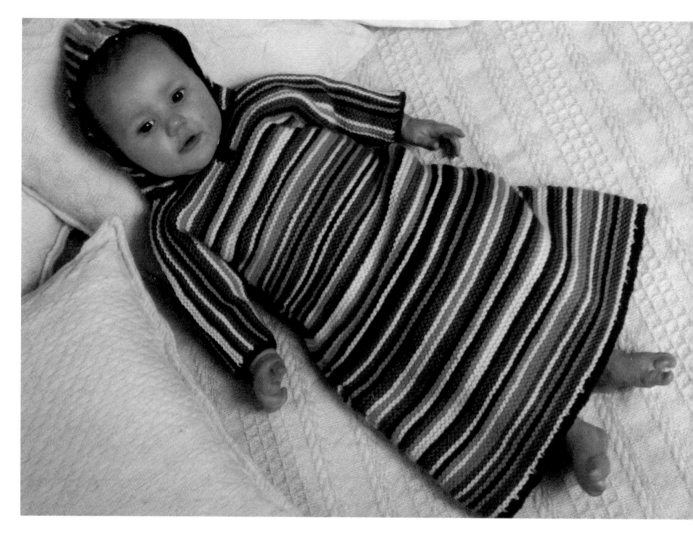

Keep baby extra-warm this winter. Knit a multicolored caftan in a simple garter stitch (knit every row) and add a single row of crochet around the hood, cuffs and bottom edge. Use washable Orlon acrylic yarns and a button shaped like a duck or other favorite animal. For extra warmth, make the caftan with a grosgrain drawstring to tie around baby's feet. As baby grows, loosen the drawstring (as shown in photograph) to let feet hang free.

INSTRUCTIONS

Sizes

Instructions are for 4- to 6-month-old baby.

Gauge

20 sts = 4"
42 rows = 4"

You need

- Two 2-oz skeins each Orlon sport yarn or 2-ply wool sport yarn in royal blue (A), white (B), medium blue (C) and orange-gold (D)
- No. 7 knitting needles (or size that will give proper gauge)
- No. 7 circular 16" knitting needle
- No. 7 double-pointed knitting needles
- Blunt yarn needle
- Size F crochet hook
- 1 animal-shaped button
- 45" gold grosgrain ribbon, ¼" wide (for optional drawstring bottom)

To make

Knit caftan in garter st in 1 piece starting at bottom front edge and ending at bottom back edge. Alternate pats 1 and 2 for front length of garment. For back of garment, reverse pat so that front and back rows will correspond when garment is folded in half for assembling.

Pat 1

2 rows A, 2 rows B, 4 rows C, 2 rows D, 2 rows A, 2 rows D, 2 rows C, 2 rows B, 2 rows C, 4 rows D, 2 rows B, 2 rows D, 2 rows A, 2 rows B, 4 rows C, 2 rows A, 4 rows B, 2 rows D, 2 rows C, 2 rows A, 2 rows B, 2 rows D, 2 rows A, 4 rows C, 2 rows B.

Pat 2

Same as pat 1 exchanging color D for A and color A for D

Front

With no. 7 needles and A, co 80.
Drawstring casement. Work 1 row in garter st. Turn and k 2 *yo, k 2 tog, k 1, yo, k 2 tog, k 3* across row 9 times, ending yo, k 2 tog, k 1, yo, k 2 tog, k 1, drop A. Attach B and begin working in pat 1 for 5", ending with wrong-side row.
Straight bottom edge. Work even in pat 1 for 1½" after co, ending with wrong-side row. Continue to work in pat, dec 1 st each side every 10 rows, 11 times. Work even in pat until piece measures 16" (19½" with casement) from beg, ending with right-side row.
Shape sleeves. At beg of next 4 rows, inc 1. At beg of next 4 rows, inc 2. At beg of next 2 rows co 10. At beg of next 2 rows, co 8. At beg of next 2 rows, co 4 — 114 sts.
Neck opening. On next row, work over 57 sts. Attach second yarn of same color and finish row. Continuing in pat, work each side separately for 2", ending with wrong-side row. During next 2 rows, bind off 6 sts at each neck edge. Continue, dec 1 each neck edge 5 times.

Back

Piece should measure approximately 7½"

from end of sleeve increases (bottom edge of sleeve opening). This is the end of Front. Repeat last 2 rows of pat color and proceed, reversing color pat for Back, working even on 46 sts each side for 6 rows. Inc 1 at each neck edge 2 times. K across wrong-side row. On next row, k across left side, co 14 and k across right side. This joins the 2 sides to finish neck opening. Continue working in pat, reversing all shapings so Back corresponds to Front (bind off where you had co, dec where you had inc, etc.)

Hood

With no. 7 circular needle, pick up 66 sts spaced evenly around entire neck edge and even with the edge of front slit. Work back and forth in pat, continuing up from neck edge evenly for 1". On next row work 26 sts, inc 1 in next st, k 5, inc 1, k 5, inc 1, k 27. Continue to work even for 6¾".
Finishing Hood. Fold in half with wrong sides tog. Break off yarn, leaving 14" end. Thread yarn through yarn needle. The knitting needle closest to you is front needle; the needle farthest from you is back needle. *Pull yarn through 1st st on front needle as if to k. Take st off needle. Pull yarn through 2nd st on front needle as if to p. Leave st on needle.* Repeat on back needle. Return to front needle and repeat from * to * beg with 1st st on front needle. This st has now been worked twice and is removed from needle. Repeat on both needles alternately. All sts except the 1st on front and back needles will be worked twice before being removed from needle. Adjust tension as you go for smooth seam.

Finishing

Sew side seams closed and weave in loose yarn ends from color changes. With size F crochet hook and A, work 1 row of sc around sleeve opening, Hood opening and neck slit, working ch-st loop at neck edge on right side of caftan for button. Sew button in place.

Drawstring

Weave ribbon through casement openings at bottom edge.

Papered Screen

Build a simple hinged screen with plywood; then give it visual excitement and a three-dimensional feel. We used marbleized papers—seen often on fine bookbindings—but you can use decorator-weight wrapping paper, wallpaper or any kind of decorative paper.

The sun, cloud, tree trunk and a shower of leaves are each cut separately and pasted on the paper "sky." Sturdy sheets of plywood hinged back and front ensure a solid standing. Use your screen as a concealer, to section off a room or simply as a dramatic viewing focus.

INSTRUCTIONS

You need

- Papered Screen Pattern (page 182)
- 4 panels ½" plywood, each 16" x 72"
- 9 flat triangular hinges with screws
- Chisel
- Hand drill
- Wire cutter
- Masking tape
- Enlarging Patterns materials (see page 206)
- 1 shirt cardboard
- 19" x 25" sheets marble or other decorative papers as follows:
    - 12 sheets blue
    - 4 sheets brown
    - 2 sheets green
    - 2 sheets green-gold
    - 1 sheet red
    - 1 sheet gold
- 1 sheet 23" x 29" white 2-ply smooth-finish paper
- Scissors
- 4" paintbrush
- 1 package cold-water wallpaper paste
- 1-2 cans clear acrylic spray

To make

1. Assembling screen. Place 4 plywood panels on floor side by side. Mark position of hinges on front along center opening (between 2nd and 3rd panels) and on back along remaining 2 openings as in Papered Screen Pattern by outlining on plywood with pencil. With chisel, rout out 1 layer of plywood inside hinge markings so hinges will lie flush with plywood and be covered by paper on screen front. Slide hinges into place; with pencil, mark screw positions. Drill a small ⅛"-deep hole for each screw. With wire cutter, cut off pointed ends of screws so they will not go all the way through plywood. Place hinges in position and screw in place. For pasting, stand screen upright and bend at hinges so papers can be pasted onto plywood edges.

2. With Enlarging Patterns Materials, bring Pattern, except for leaves, up to full size. Allow 1" space all around grid. Cut drawing apart to make paper pattern for tree trunk, sun, cloud and border strips. With Enlarging Patterns Materials and cardboard, bring 1 or 2 leaves up to full size; cut patterns.

3. With wallpaper paste and paintbrush, cover entire surface of plywood screen panels with blue paper. Overlap paper onto plywood edges and around to back. Let dry. With cardboard pattern, cut leaves from green and green-gold papers. Cut tree trunk, sun, cloud and border strips from remaining papers as indicated in Pattern; allow ½" for overlapping onto plywood edges. Piece papers where necessary.

4. With wallpaper paste, paste cutouts on screen over blue paper positioned as in Pattern, in the following order: border strips, tree trunk, sun, cloud and leaves.

5. Spray entire surface of finished screen with 2 coats clear acrylic spray.

Silver Jewelry

Add elegance to your most casual denims and accent your best party clothes with this collection of truly American jewelry. The sterling silver sheets and the few metalworking tools you'll need are available from jewelry-making suppliers; the rest of the materials can be purchased at any hardware store.

Molding silver into exciting designs like these is easy, too. Silver is a pliable metal that can be cut, shaped, drilled and hammered to make any and all of these exquisite pieces. Make some extras; jewelry is so often the ideal gift.

LINK NECKLACE INSTRUCTIONS

You need

- 3" x 6" piece 22-gauge sterling silver sheet
- Metal-cutting shears
- Needle file
- Emery board
- Block of soft wood
- Sharp nail
- Hammer
- Electric drill with ⅟16" metal drill bit
- 2-3 dozen sterling silver jump rings
- Chain-nose pliers
- Silver polish and soft cloth

To make

1. With metal-cutting shears, cut silver sheet into ⅜" x 6" strips of random lengths from ¾" to 1¼". File and smooth all edges with needle file and emery board.

2. Place 1 metal piece on wooden block. Place point of nail on end of piece, centered and ³⁄16" from end; tap nail with hammer to mark position of hole on silver piece; repeat on other end of piece. Repeat with all silver pieces. Drill holes in all pieces where marked.

3. With twisting motion, open jump rings. With ends of jump ring facing up, place 1 silver piece on each end of ring with dull surface facing up. Close all rings; closures should all be on wrong side of necklace. Link pairs together in same manner. With pliers,

squeeze ends of each ring together to secure. Clean necklace with polish and soft cloth.

SILVER PENDANT INSTRUCTIONS

You need

- ½ to ¾ oz. sterling silver scrap
- Charcoal block
- Propane torch
- Ice cream or other small wooden stick
- Chain-nose pliers
- Empty can
- Tarnish-removing silver cleaner
- Old toothbrush
- Sheet of smooth metal scrap
- Planishing hammer (optional)
- Manual or electric drill with ⅟16" metal drill bit
- Needle file or nail file
- Silver polish
- Soft cloth
- 1 silver jump ring
- ½ oz. liquid silver
- Nylon fishline
- Epoxy glue

To make

1. Place ½" tarnish-removing silver cleaner in can. Set aside.

2. Place silver scrap on charcoal block. Place block on concrete or stone surface. Direct flame of torch at scrap on block until scrap turns red and liquefies. To alter shape of melted silver, turn torch flame away and poke at silver with wooden stick to reshape it. If stick catches fire, blow it out and continue reshaping. Repeat until desired shape is attained, then turn off torch.

3. As soon as silver solidifies (10 seconds), pick it up with pliers and throw it into can containing silver cleaner. Silver will sizzle. Leave in cleaner 5 minutes; remove with pliers. If silver is still dirty, scrub with toothbrush; pendant will have domed surface and dull silver color.

4. If desired, flatten surface of pendant by placing pendant on flat metal scrap on concrete floor and hitting pendant with flat end of planishing hammer. Drill hole in pendant at desired point. With file, smooth away burrs along pendant edges. Clean with polish and soft cloth.

5. Insert jump ring through hole; close. Thread liquid silver on fishline to desired length, making sure necklace fits over head. Thread pendant on liquid silver necklace. Tie fishline ends together in knot as close as possible to liquid silver. Trim ends close to knot and secure knot by dabbing with epoxy glue.

HAMMERED CUFF INSTRUCTIONS

You need

- 3" x 6" piece 22-gauge sterling silver sheet
- Metal-cutting shears
- Needle file
- Emery board
- 12" square 1"-thick perfectly smooth soft wood
- Felt-tip marker
- Ruler
- 3"-long smooth dome-shaped bolt
- Heavy hammer
- Metal scouring pad (optional)
- Silver polish and soft cloth
- 2"-diameter straight-sided glass jar

To make

1. With metal-cutting shears, cut 2" x 5½" strip from silver sheet. With needle file, file edges and corners of strip with rounding motion. Finish smoothing edges with emery board.

2. Place wooden square on firm work surface. Place strip, shiny side down, on wood. With felt-tip marker, draw a straight line ⅜" from and parallel to each long edge. Mark 7 dots along each line at ¾" intervals beginning and ending dots ½" from each short edge; the 4th dot along each line will be in center of bracelet

(14 dots total). Place dome end of bolt on 1 dot, holding bolt firmly in hand; strike bolt with hammer to make slight impression in silver; repeat on all dots. Repeat striking on all dots once or twice more or until desired depth of impressions is attained. Check for scratches on shiny side of silver. To remove scratches, stroke with metal scouring pad in direction of scratch only until it disappears. With polish, clean entire surface. Repeat scouring and cleaning if necessary.

3. Shaping cuff. Stand silver on edge next to jar with raised side away from jar. Form strip into U-shape (see Fig. 1) around jar with hands. If silver is difficult to bend, put strip on burner of gas range, turn on burner and leave for 5 minutes. Turn off burner; let strip cool completely. Repeat shaping process. Place hand around U-shape; cup hand and squeeze U-shape closed (Fig. 2). Repeat with other side, leaving ¾" gap between edges. With polish, polish cuff.

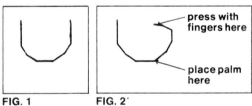

FIG. 1   FIG. 2

AZTEC CUFF INSTRUCTIONS

You need

- 3" x 6" piece 22-gauge sterling silver sheet
- Metal-cutting shears
- Needle file
- Emery board
- 1"-thick 12"-square wooden block
- Felt-tip marker
- Ruler
- Manual or electric drill with 1/16" metal drill bit
- Scissors
- Two 18"-24" strands 18-gauge round sterling silver wire
- Chain-nose pliers (optional)
- Silver solder (optional)
- Propane torch (optional)
- 2"-diameter straight-sided glass jar
- Metal scouring pad (optional)
- Silver polish
- Soft cloth
- Velour towel or other napped cloth
- Old soft-bristle toothbrush

To make

1. With metal-cutting shears, cut 1½" x 5½" strip from silver sheet. Finish edges as in step 1, Hammered Cuff Instructions.

2. Place wooden square on firm work surface. Place silver strip on wood, shiny side down. With felt-tip marker, mark dots on dull side of silver strip (Fig. 3). With drill, drill holes in strip at dots. Enlarge holes shown by larger dots in Fig. 3 by inserting 1 scissors blade and twisting it in hole; enlarge center hole so 4 wires will fit in it; enlarge remaining large-dot holes so 2 wires will fit. Insert wires to check sizes of holes.

3. File both ends of both strands of silver wire; smooth with emery board. Hold wire with thumb and forefinger, leaving a 1" tail, then thread 1st strand through holes in strip as in Fig. 4. When wire curves up above surface of strip, smooth down by pressing wire with thumb where it comes out of the hole in the direction of the next hole; this helps keep wire

straight. When threading is complete, trim wire to leave 1" tail. With pliers, wind the 2 ends around threaded wires to secure. Repeat process, threading 2nd strand as shown in Fig. 5. If desired, solder wire ends in place with silver solder. If wires on shiny side of strip are not flush, take up slack by gently twisting wire from wrong side with pliers.

4. Form strip around jar as in step 3 of Hammered Cuff Instructions; remove scratches as in step 2. With polish, towel and toothbrush, clean bracelet.

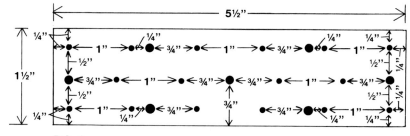

FIG. 3

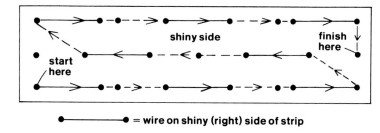

= wire on shiny (right) side of strip

= wire on dull (wrong) side of strip

FIG. 4
THREADING STRIPES

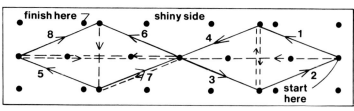

FIG. 5
THREADING DIAMOND DESIGNS

Seminole
Stitched Apron

Seminole Indian women obtained scraps of cotton fabric, cut squares from the odd-shaped remnants and stitched the squares together in bright patchwork patterns. They then sewed the whole design to a solid-color backing.

In this apron we've modified and modernized the Seminole technique by using stripes of bias tape and hem facing to achieve the same effect. The stripes are stuffed with polyester fiber to give them an additional dimension and the entire apron is machine-stitched.

INSTRUCTIONS

You need

- Seminole Apron Pattern (page 183)
- Enlarging Patterns materials (see page 206)
- ½ yd. 45"-wide purple heavyweight cotton fabric
- ½ yd. unbleached muslin
- 2"-wide polyester/cotton hem facing:
    2 pkgs. purple
    1 pkg. each red, copper, navy, tan and black
- Single-fold bias tape:
    1 pkg. purple in ½" width
    1 pkg. each red, copper and black in 1" width
- Thread to match hem facings and bias tapes
- Sewing machine zipper foot
- ¼ lb. polyester fiber stuffing
- 4 yds. ⅝" wide black fold-over braid
- Knitting needle
- 4 hooks and eyes

To make

Preshrink hem facings, bias tapes, fabrics and fold-over braid before cutting by dipping in hot water and allowing to dry. Apron is purple, designs on it are piecework.

Bring Seminole Apron Pattern up to full size, adding ½" seam allowances to top and bottom edges of bib, all 4 edges of waistband and top edge of skirt. Cut 1 Collar, 1 Bib, 2 Waistbands (1 is facing) and 1 Skirt from purple fabric. Cut 1 Collar and 1 Skirt from muslin.

Collar

Stitch together strips of hem facing and bias tape along folds with right sides together in order and colors shown in photograph to form Collar piecework. Begin at center front with 2" purple hem facing and work first to the right side, then to the left. Hand stitch a strip of ½" red bias tape to center of purple center-front strip. Trim stitched piecework to same size as muslin Collar. Stitch to muslin Collar ½" from edge, leaving openings at ends of each 1" copper strip at center front. With zipper foot and thread to match copper, carefully stitch along seamline on each side of each copper strip through strip and muslin. Do not stitch ends. Stuff small amount of polyester fiber stuffing between copper strip and muslin. Stitch closed ½" from edge. With wrong sides together, stitch muslin Collar to purple Collar ½" from edge. Bind all Collar edges with fold-over braid by topstitching in place.

Bib

Machine- or hand-stitch 1" red bias tape to right side of purple Bib positioned as in Seminole Apron Pattern. Bind side edges with fold-over braid by topstitching in place.

Waistband

Stitch together 27½" strips of bias tape as in Fig. 1. Cut stitched strips into 2½" pieces. Pin pieces together to form strips as in Fig. 2, offsetting colors so that strip forms a diagonal "step" design. Stitch strips together in ¼" seam allowances and press seams open. Stitch piecework to right side of 1 waistband along edges. Trim off excess piecework even with waistband. With right sides together stitch Waistband to Waistband facing in ½" seam allowance, leaving 8" openings centered along top and bottom edges for inserting Bib and Skirt later. Turn to right side; press.

Skirt

For vertical piecework on top half of Skirt, stitch together strips along folds with right sides together in order shown in photograph. Stitch piecework to top half of muslin Skirt ½" from edge, leaving openings at ends of red and navy strips. Stitch and stuff red and navy strips as in Collar instructions, using knitting needle to distribute stuffing evenly. Using method in Waistband instructions and 20" strips of hem facing, stitch together purple-copper-navy-tan piecework as in photograph, and piecework identical to waistband for bottom edge.

Assembling skirt

Starting with 2" black hem facing at center of skirt, stitch together strips and pieceworks along folds with right sides together positioned as in Seminole Apron Pattern. Press seams open. Stitch top edge of center black strip to bottom edge of stuffed Skirt piecework through all layers with right sides together. Stitch lower half of Skirt piecework to muslin ½" from edge. With wrong sides together, stitch muslin Skirt to purple Skirt along all edges ½" from edge. Bind side and bottom edges with fold-over braid.

Assembling apron

Zigzag top edge of Bib. Place Collar over this edge and topstitch in place through fold-over braid. Insert Bib and Skirt in Waistband openings and topstitch in place. Try on for fit. Stitch 2 hooks and eyes to Collar back and 2 hooks and eyes to Waistband back.   ○

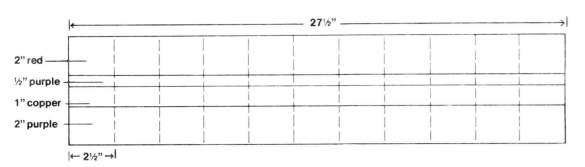

FIG. 1
STITCHING WAISTBAND PIECEWORK STRIPS

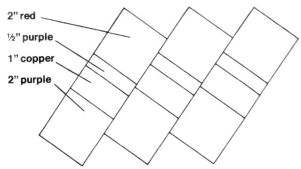

FIG. 2
DIAGONAL DESIGN

Cyanotype Quilt

Favorite photographs reproduced in blue-and-white cyanotypes are an integral part of this satin quilt. The cyanotype process dates back to 1842 and was originally used for making building blueprints. Two safe crystalline chemicals, your favorite photo negatives, natural sunlight and fabric with high natural-fiber content are all it takes to produce beautiful cyanotype prints for this quilt. Chemicals for the process are available at photographic-supply shops. Use cyanotype printing to transfer images from negatives to T-shirts, pillowcases, curtains, scarves or prints to be framed as well.

A regular 9" x 12" negative can be used, but the high contrast of Kodalith negatives gives the best results. Kodalith negatives can be made from black-and-white snapshot negatives by a photo-processing laboratory. The same negative can be used to make any number of prints.

CYANOTYPE PRINTING INSTRUCTIONS

You need

- Rubber gloves
- 1 oz. ferric ammonium citrate crystals
- ½ cup water
- ½ oz. potassium ferricyanide
- 2 brown glass bottles
- 1¼ yds. 45"-wide white polished cotton (50%-100% cotton without permanent-press finish)
- Glass mixing bowl
- 2" paintbrush
- 2 sheets ⅛" glass, 12" x 15" each
- One 9" x 12" black-and-white Kodalith negative for each image you wish to reproduce

To make

1. Wear rubber gloves while working with chemicals. Mix together 1 oz. ferric ammonium citrate and ½ cup water; stir until crystals dissolve. Do the same with ½ oz. potassium ferricyanide and ½ cup water. Store each solution in a separate brown glass bottle until ready to use (solutions may be stored separately up to 4 months).

2. Cut polished cotton into twelve 11" x 14" rectangles (Fig. 1).

3. In a darkened room, stir together equal parts (about 2 tablespoons each) of 2 solutions in mixing bowl. With paintbrush, coat right (shiny) side of each fabric rectangle as evenly as possible with mixed solution; coat in groups of 1-3, then mix more coating. Coated fabric will turn chartreuse. Let dry in a dark place; fabric will appear brighter chartreuse after drying. Coated fabric should be printed within 6 hours or chemicals will lose their effectiveness.

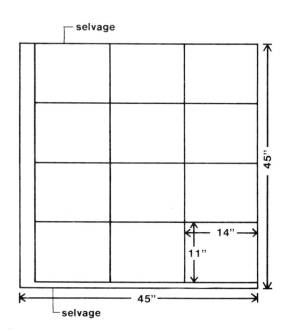

selvage

45"

14"

11"

45"

selvage

**FIG. 1
PRINT LAYOUT**

4. Assemble dried coated fabric, glass sheets and negative(s) in the darkened room. Place 1 fabric rectangle, coated side up, on 1 glass sheet. Place 1 negative, emulsion (dull) side down, atop fabric. Top with 2nd glass sheet so negative makes good contact with fabric. Place the glass-fabric package outside in <u>direct</u> sunlight on a dry surface. When image turns charcoal blue, print is properly exposed. This will happen very quickly in summer sunlight but could take as long as 1 hour in less-intense sunlight. Take package inside, remove the fabric and rinse it 3-10 minutes in slightly lukewarm running water until all chartreuse color is gone. Let print dry indoors. Repeat process with each negative you wish to print to get a total of 12 prints. When prints are dry, you may wash them in soap, iron them or have them dry cleaned; do not use bleach.

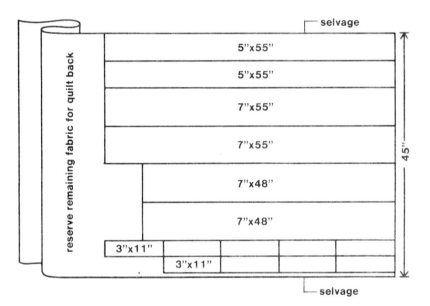

QUILT INSTRUCTIONS

You need

- 3⅝ yds. 45"-wide white fleece-back satin or polished cotton
- Dressmaker's pencil
- Twelve 11" x 14" cyanotype prints
- White thread
- 1 piece 42" x 61" puffy polyester batting

To make

Use ½" seam allowance on all seams.

1. Cut satin strips as follows for quilt front: nine 3" x 11", two 7" x 55", two 5" x 55", two 7" x 48". Reserve remaining satin for quilt back (Fig. 2).

2. With dressmaker's pencil, mark seamlines on cyanotype prints to outline 9" x 12" rectangles. Trim seam allowances to ½" (rectangles should measure 10" x 13"). Arrange rectangles in 3 rows of 4 prints each.

3. Insert 3" x 11" strips between 4 prints in a lengthwise row. Stitch prints and strips together. Repeat with 2 more groups of 4 prints and remaining 3" x 11" strips to make 3 total lengthwise rows of 4 prints each.

4. Stitch one 5" x 55" strip between the left and middle rows and another between middle and right rows. Stitch one 7" x 55" strip to each remaining unstitched lengthwise seam allowance to form side border. Stitch 1 each 7" x 48" strip to top and bottom edge to form borders.

5. Quilting. Set sewing machine foot at a very low pressure and stitch length at 6 stitches per inch; practice with scraps of satin and batting before stitching quilt. With right side up, place quilt front atop batting. Beginning at center and working out to edges, pin, then machine stitch through front and batting along all seamlines. Quilt border last by machine stitching in leaf pattern. Quilt front should measure about 42" x 61" when quilting is complete.

6. Cut quilt back from reserved satin using quilt front as a pattern. With right sides together, stitch front to back in ½" seam, leaving a 24" opening along one 42" edge. Trim seam allowance to ¼", clip across corners and turn to right side. Whipstitch opening closed. To secure front to back, hand tack with white thread through all layers at all 4 corners of each print.

**FIG. 2.
SATIN LAYOUT**

Needlepoint
Ornaments

Just one-fourth yard of 10-mesh canvas makes six traditional Christmas ornaments that add a special, personal touch to your tree. Work the ornaments entirely in cross-stitch, using Persian yarn with pearl cotton and metallic threads to highlight; then sew the canvas to a piece of felt. Stuff the ornament, complete the stitching, add cord or yarn for hanging and give a bright welcome to the holiday season.

INSTRUCTIONS

You need

- Ornament Patterns (pages 184-185)
- ¼ yd. Penelope 10-mesh needlepoint canvas
- Persian yarn in the following colors:

dark navy blue	light peach
medium blue	pale yellow
red	brown
gold	beige
dark green	purple
light green	lavender
rust	white

- Size 8 pearl cotton in light blue, bright gold and bright green
- Silver metallic thread
- Size 18 tapestry needle
- ¼ yd. felt
- Needle and thread
- 1 bag polyester fiber stuffing
- 1 knitting needle
- Decorative accessories (optional)

To make

2 yds. yarn worked in cross-stitch covers 1 sq. in. of canvas.

1. With 2 strands of 3-strand Persian yarn or double strand of pearl cotton thread, work ornaments in cross-stitch according to designs in Ornament Patterns.

2. After needlepoint is complete, trim canvas to ¼" seam allowance around each design; turn seam allowance to wrong side, clipping curves and angles almost to stitching where necessary for smooth contour.

3. With needle and thread, overcast design around edge to a piece of felt, leaving 1" opening for stuffing. Trim excess felt along overcasting. With tapestry needle and yarn in same shade as border of needlepoint, overcast edge of ornament except at opening, covering edge completely.

4. Stuff ornament with polyester fiber stuffing, using a knitting needle to work stuffing into all contours of ornament. Stitch opening closed with needle and thread; overcast as in step 3.

5. Sew a length of cord or yarn to top of each ornament, checking for balance when ornament dangles. If desired, stitch the following accessories to ornaments: tiny artificial flowers and wrapped present to hands of Strollers; artificial flower to Musician's hair; silver threads and sequins to Musician's guitar; leather strip and 3 golden beads to necks of Leopard and Reindeer; feather to Horseman's hat; cord to Horseman's hand for reins. ○

Sand Casting

Change plaster and sand into a work of art that takes only a morning to create. Use just one large object or design a grouping of many small ones to make the impression for your sculpture. Choose a number of different items from your kitchen shelf; embed some buttons, stones, seashells or empty spools, then make your pour. Plaster of Paris does the work.

Do not use very large objects in sand casting. As the plaster dries, it will shrink and cause cracking. However, as long as you leave a little space between small items, incorporate as many of them into your design as you choose. The shrinkage around them will be insignificant.

When you hang your casting, position it so that slanting light shadows the impressions into bold relief.

INSTRUCTIONS

You need

- 1 wooden box
- 1 wooden board cut to width that fits snugly inside box
- Damp sand
- Trowel, fork and other impression-making implements
- Sea shells, stones, buttons or other small decorative objects
- Plaster of Paris
- Bucket
- Stick
- Twine (optional)

To make

1. Fill box with sand, allowing enough room above sand for desired thickness of casting. Smooth sand. Slide wooden board into box to create desired width of casting (see Fig. 1). With hands or impression-making implements, form desired design in sand. If sand becomes too dry, sprinkle a little water over it to dampen. Embed decorative objects in sand until desired design is complete (Fig. 2).

2. Mix plaster of Paris in bucket according to package directions to consistency of heavy cream. Splash plaster very carefully into crevices and cracks of design (Fig. 3); then gently pour plaster over entire sand surface. If you splash too hard or pour too fast the sudden weight of the plaster will distort the design.

3. When enough plaster has been poured that the casting is about half the finished thickness, place a twine loop in plaster for hanging, if desired. Cut a generous length of twine and tie a loose loop in either end of it. Place the prepared twine in the center of the casting near the top. Position it so that the twine between the 2 loops will not be embedded in the plaster when the pour is completed (Fig. 4).

4. After you have placed the twine, pour additional plaster to desired thickness (Fig. 5). Make sure portion of twine for hanging casting is free of the plaster.

5. Let casting dry until it is hard enough to lift (about 1 hour). Remove board to expose edge of partly dry casting (Fig. 6) and lift casting out (Fig. 7). Casting will be coated with sand. Let casting dry completely (several hours); then brush away excess sand (see Fig. 8).

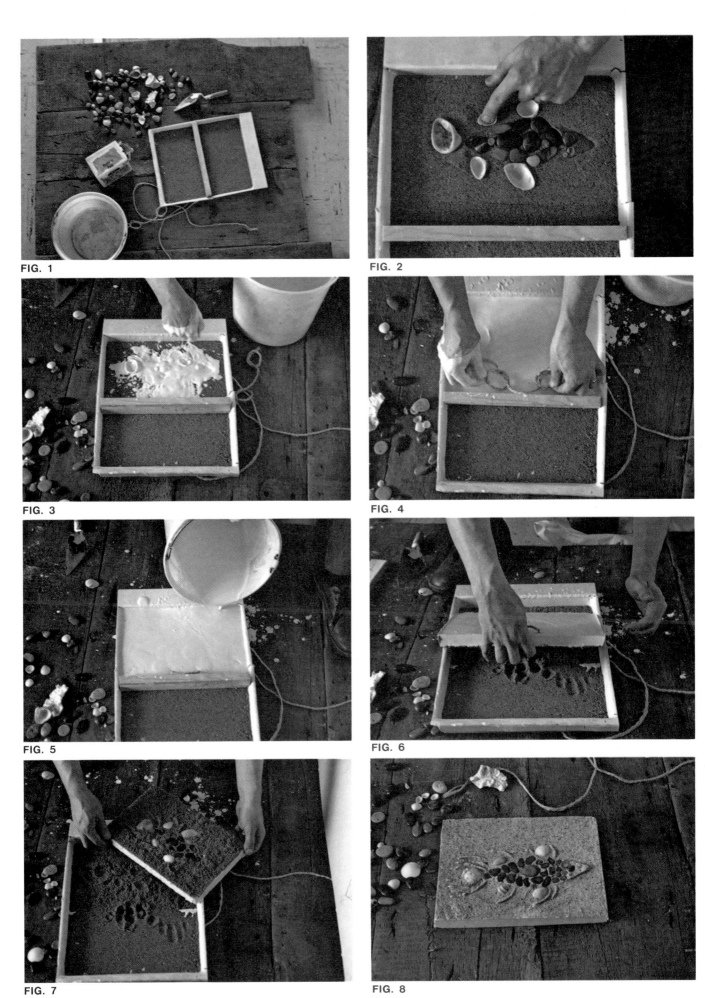

FIG. 1

FIG. 2

FIG. 3

FIG. 4

FIG. 5

FIG. 6

FIG. 7

FIG. 8

Dollhouse

You're never too big to enjoy a dollhouse, especially this open and airy one that's specially designed for easy "playability." Built on legs so your child won't have to bend almost double to use its first floor, the dollhouse's rooms are shallow enough so that arranging and rearranging furniture is simplified. Parents will enjoy keeping an eye out while shopping for unusual miniatures and dollhouse furniture, as well as making many of the accessories from fabric, carpet or tile scraps or samples. Variety stores and museum shops are just two excellent sources for all kinds of dollhouse decorating helps.

Construct the house with thin plywood, nails and heavy-duty tape. Roof it with cardboard shingles and cover the walls with gesso; then add wall and floor coverings made from scraps. All the supplies you'll need are available at hardware, art-supply and lumber-supply stores.

Plan the rooms around your child's special interests—add a science lab, music room, ballroom, exercise area, guest room or bedroom for the grandparents, and more. Your dollhouse is sure to become a cherished heirloom for generations to come.

INSTRUCTIONS

You need

- Saber saw
- Sawhorses
- One 4' x 8' sheet ¼" plywood
- Contact cement
- 1 box ¾" finishing nails
- 1 roll duct tape
- 12' unfinished ½" inside corner molding
- 6' unfinished ¾" outside corner molding
- Miter box (optional)
- 1 kit 4 unfinished 9"-tall wooden table legs with brackets and screws
- Artist's knife or scissors
- 3 sq. ft. ¹⁄₁₆"-thick cardboard or illustration board
- 1 pint white gesso
- Paintbrush
- 1 pint each quick-drying green and red enamel paint

To make

1. With saber saw and sawhorses, cut dollhouse pieces from plywood (Fig. 1).

2. With plywood pieces, contact cement and nails, assemble dollhouse as follows: Attach sides to back with back overlapping sides; from outside, drive nails through back into sides along nail lines (see Fig. 1). Cement 2 bottom pieces together to form ½"-thick bottom. Attach bottom to back, with bottom overlapping back. Nail bottom to sides through bottom.

3. <u>Roof.</u> Tape roof back and roof front together with duct tape so roof will fit over peaks in sides. Cut top strip of tape slightly longer than roof width and overlap to finish edge. Place roof over top of house; cement to sides and nail through roof. Tape back edge where roof and back meet from inside and outside of house.

4. Cut inside corner trim molding into three 27¾" strips and six 10" strips. Cut ends of molding strips at a 45° angle so they will meet smoothly and squarely in corners (use miter box, if desired). Cement 1 long strip and 2 short strips to back and sides of house on the inside to form a platform for the 2nd floor. Make sure top edge of molding is 10" from bottom of house. Cement 2nd floor to molding. Repeat process, placing 3rd floor 10" above 2nd floor and attic 8½" above 3rd floor.

5. Trim away top corners on each wall piece to accommodate molding. Insert walls to form rooms as desired (see photograph). Cut two 30" strips outside corner molding; cement to back corners of house vertically to finish corner.

6. Attach legs to bottom corners of house, following kit directions.

7. With artist's knife or scissors, cut rectangular shingles of various sizes with rounded corners from cardboard or illustration board. Cement to top of roof one at a time in uneven rows. Start at bottom and overlap roof edge with 1st row of shingles. Overlap each row with the next row until shingles reach top edge. Finish off top edge with duct tape.

8. Paint entire roof surface (shingles) and inside of house with gesso; let dry. Paint outside with green enamel and roof with 2-3 coats red enamel.

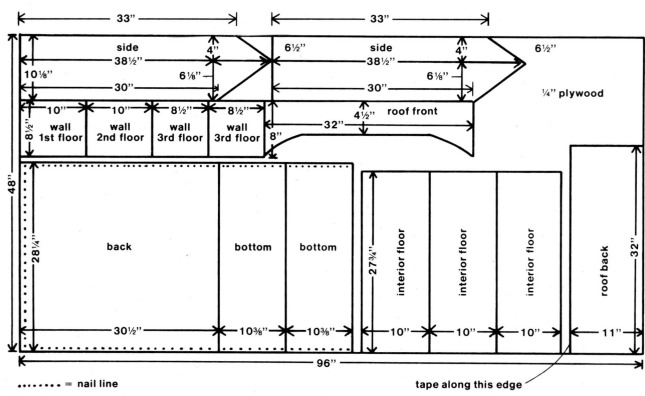

.... = nail line

tape along this edge

FIG. 1
DOLLHOUSE LAYOUT

Paintbrush Batik Quilt

Two historic crafts, batik and patchwork, are mated in dramatic harmony on this sunset-colored quilt.

Batik is an East Indian method of coloring fabric. Parts of the fabric are covered with wax to resist coloration when the whole piece is immersed in a dye bath. In this quilt, old-fashioned American-style patchwork highlights the batik colors and patterns. Cut the patchwork squares from cotton sheets; never use permanent press or synthetic fabrics as they do not take dyes well. Be sure the fabric has been washed at least once in hot, sudsy water to remove all factory sizings.

The colors in this quilt were achieved by dyeing the squares in successive dye baths of different colors and applying wax (paraffin) between the baths. Some squares are dyed in solid colors; others are batiked in a succession of three colors. Do not use metal containers for dyeing. Use an artist's brush to apply melted wax in geometric shapes to the squares before dyeing in each dye bath. To melt the paraffin, place it in a clean soup can in a saucepan of water set on a hot plate or range. Keep the water level at least equal to the wax level, and keep the water boiling gently.

When you've completed the dyeing process, iron the wax out of the batiked fabric between layers of newspaper and paper toweling, replacing the paper as it absorbs the melted wax. Then stitch the squares together in an arrangement that integrates prints with solids to form the quilt top.

INSTRUCTIONS

You need

- 1 or more old 100% cotton sheet(s)
- ½ oz. each yellow, red and blue cold-water, colorfast dyes
- Non-metal dye bath container
- Non-metal stirrers for dyes
- Rubber gloves (optional)
- Clothesline
- 1 package paraffin
- Old saucepan or electric frying pan
- Natural bristle artist's paintbrush
- Waxed paper, paper towel and newspaper
- Iron
- Cleaning solvent (optional)
- Thread to match dyed squares
- Washable double-bed-sized blanket or two 72" x 84" layers of polyester batting
- Double-bed-sized cotton sheet in coordinating color
- Embroidery pearl cotton to match dyed squares
- Embroidery needle(s)

To batik

Instructions for 2 possible dye progressions are given so you can create your own color schemes. Dyes in the 2nd dye progression are given in [   ]. Dye some squares with the 1st set of colors listed and some with the 2nd. Wear rubber gloves if desired.

1. Tear or cut cotton sheet(s) into forty-two 13" squares. Mix yellow [very pale red] dye according to package instructions. (If desired, add small amount of red dye to yellow while dyes are in powder state for orange-yellow.) Dye all squares in this dye bath according to package directions. Hang squares on clothesline to dry. Set aside 3 to 4 squares to be used as solids in patchwork. Reserve 3 to 4 additional squares to be dyed solid in 2nd dye bath and 3 to 4 additional squares to be dyed solid in both 2nd and 3rd dye baths. All other squares will be batiked.

2. Melt paraffin in saucepan on range or hot plate. Place several layers of newspaper on work surface, top with waxed paper, then 1 yellow square. With paintbrush, apply melted paraffin to square in simple geometric shapes positioned where you want yellow color to remain. When paraffin is dry, turn square over and apply paraffin to 2nd side exactly where it was applied to 1st side. Wax should appear transparent when both waxings are complete. Repeat for all squares to be batiked.

3. When wax is dry, dip squares in clean, cool water to saturate fabric so it can accept dye evenly. Mix red [yellow] dye bath. Dye waxed squares and 6 to 8 unwaxed squares in this dye bath. Hang squares on line to dry. You now have 2 colors on squares. Wax those areas on waxed squares where you want 2nd color to remain, as in step 2.

4. Mix blue [blue-red] dye bath. Repeat dyeing and drying step, adding 3 to 4 unwaxed squares that were dyed in both 1st and 2nd dye baths; do not wax before dyeing. When dry, wax over any unwaxed areas on batiked squares. Let wax harden.

5. Place ¼" to ½" layer of newspaper on work surface; top with paper towel. Place 1 square on paper towel; top with another paper towel and single layer of newspaper. With dry iron at medium setting, press square to remove wax. Replace paper layers as they absorb wax. Some wax will remain; batik will be slightly stiff. To soften batik, if desired, soak it in a tube of cleaning solvent, stir occasionally and remove when batik feels soft, about 10 minutes. Always use solvent outside or in a well-ventilated area. Blot batik between 2 old bath towels.

To make quilt

1. Arrange waxed and solid squares on floor in desired 6-square x 7-square pattern. Stitch squares together in ½" seams as follows: Stitch the 1st row of squares together end to end. Repeat with each remaining row. Stitch rows together, matching seams for precise patchwork. Quilt top is now complete.

2. Stitch blanket to wrong side of backing sheet. With right side of top facing right side of backing sheet, stitch layers together ½" from quilt edges. Leave a 24" opening along 1 straight edge for turning. For smooth corners, gently curve stitching at corners and clip. Turn to right side, whipstitch opening closed. Tuft quilt by tacking all layers together with pearl cotton at corners of squares. Cut ends of tacking should be on back (solid) side of quilt. For first laundering, rinse quilt in cold water. Then wash in warm water and mild suds; line dry.

Wood Sculpture

Two raven-haired tumblers, suited in scarlet and green, clasp hands in this joyful puzzle that perches on a simple wooden base. The pieces interlock snugly with precisely meshing curves and grooves.

You need no special skills or tools—just white pine, a jig or coping saw, sandpaper, glue, paints and varnish. Acrylic paints are the best; they dry flat and permanent and they mellow beautifully on wood.

The finished sculpture is 12½" x 7¼".

INSTRUCTIONS

You need

- Wood Sculpture Pattern (page 186)
- Large piece of paper
- Ruler
- Pencil
- 12" x 14" piece of ½"-thick white pine
- Jigsaw with fine blade (10-12 teeth per inch) or coping saw and C-clamp
- #220 sandpaper
- Acrylic paints in green, red, black, blue and white
- Artist's paintbrush
- Clear varnish or shellac
- Wood-bonding glue

To make

1. With ruler and pencil, draw grid of 1" squares on paper. Draw design on new grid exactly as they appear in Wood Sculpture Pattern. Draw base separately as it will be cut separately.

2. Turn drawing over; rub side of pencil point over paper to create "carbon paper." Place drawing on pine, carbon side down, and draw over all lines, including details. Lift up drawing; design should be transferred to pine. Repeat for base.

3. With saw, cut design from pine, around design first then between hands, then interior cut-outs. (If using coping saw, clamp pine to work table with C-clamp.) Cut base from pine. Sand all pieces lightly to smooth edges, making sure pieces fit together easily but snugly. Do not sand flat bottom edge of design.

4. If necessary, redraw details on pine. With 2 coats acrylic paint and artist's paintbrush, paint sculpture according to colors in Pattern. Let dry. With wood-bonding glue, glue bottom edge of sculpture to center of base. Let set. With artist's paintbrush, apply 1 or 2 coats varnish to sculpture and base.

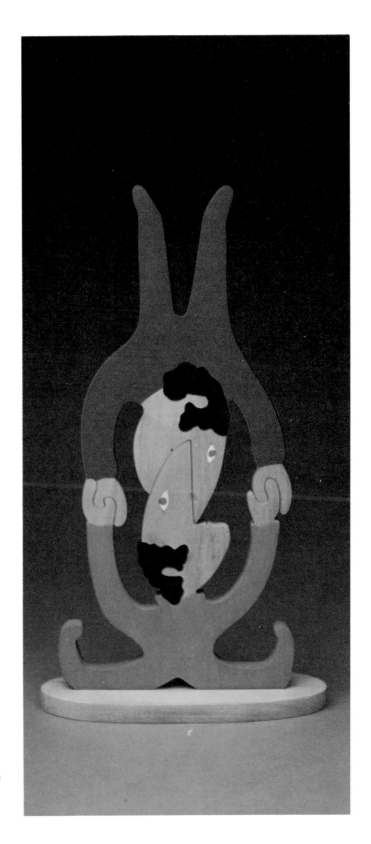

Preserved Flowers

With tiny silica-gel crystals, available wherever florist supplies are sold, you can preserve the beauty of fresh or cut flowers for years on end. Silica gel is a highly absorbent substance ideal for preserving flowers. The procedure is simple: Cover flowers for a few days in silica-gel crystals enclosed in an airtight container, so water can evaporate without destroying the flowers' natural beauty. Once the flowers are dry, spray them with a fixative, arrange them into a bouquet—and enjoy them for a long, long time.

Silica-gel crystals can be used over and over again for season after season of dried flowers. Indicator crystals turn pink or white when your silica gel has absorbed as much moisture as it can hold. Place it in a 250° oven for three hours and the indicator crystals will turn blue again—ready to preserve more flowers. To insure maximum usefulness, always store new and reactivated silica gel in an airtight container.

INSTRUCTIONS

You need

- Flower blooms or buds
- #26 or #28 florist's wire
- Silica-gel crystals in sufficient amount to cover selected flowers
- Clear plastic closet box or cookie tin
- Saltshaker (optional)
- Masking tape
- Small camel's-hair artist's brush
- Small cloth bag
- White glue (optional)
- Floral-arranging stem wires
- Florist's tape
- Clear dried-material preservative spray

To make

Preparation

Choose flowers at the peak of bloom and when they are completely dry. If you choose line flowers, break clusters into single blooms before drying. Red and purple blooms are not recommended; they often fade in the drying process. Cut stem off 1"-2" below bud. Insert #26 or #28 florist's wire crosswise through stem just beneath bloom. Draw wire through so both ends are even, fold ends down hairpin-style and twist them together to form a strong artificial stem (Fig. 1). If natural stem is fairly thick, push wire directly up natural stem (Fig. 2). Prepare extras.

FIG. 1   **FIG. 2**

Drying

Dry only 1 type of flower at a time in each container. Pour 1"-2" silica-gel crystals into bottom of container. Carefully place blooms atop crystals. Bend wire stems at right angles and stick them into the silica gel so the flowers are atop crystals but do not touch each other (Fig. 3). Gently mound crystals up underneath each bloom for support, then slowly sift more silica gel over blooms until they are entirely covered. If blooms are very delicate, sprinkle crystals on blooms with saltshaker. When all blooms are covered, add silica gel to bury blooms under a ½"-1" layer of crystals. Cover container, seal with tape and record the date and the type of flower you are preserving.

Timing

Drying time varies from 1 to 5 days and depends on humidity, the amount of water in the bloom and the moisture in your silica gel. In general, heavier blooms take a longer time. When you think a bloom is dry, gently pour off top layer of silica gel and carefully brush away any remaining crystals. Remove bloom and brush away all clinging crystals. If you have miscalculated and bloom is not yet dry, replace it in the crystals; if it is nearly dry, put it on the surface of the silica gel. Reseal the box.

Storage and Display

Store dried blooms in airtight box with a small cloth bag containing a few tablespoons of silica gel. With white glue, replace any petals that fall off. To prepare flowers for arranging, bind another wire to the stem with florist's tape. Spray each bloom with clear dried-material preservative, or keep arrangement under a dome or in glass-enclosed frame.   ○

SUGGESTED FLOWERS AND FLORA

African violet

Carnation

Clematis

Clover

Crab apples

Dandelion

Feverfew

Hen and Chickens

Lavender

Leaves from trees

Marigold

Mushrooms

Pansy

Phlox

Queen Anne's lace

Rose

Tulip tree blossoms

Wild bloodroot

FIG. 3

Crochet Bedspread

Rows of circular motifs in thin cotton cord worked with a tiny hook create a delicate bedspread that has lacy, old-fashioned charm.

Work the large and small motifs in rounds and join them together in rows as they are completed. Work in thread ends as you go. Use the spread in a traditional Early American bedroom, a room patterned after the 1930s or '40s or any eclectically decorated room. The same motifs in smaller groupings make lovely table runners, placemats or dresser scarves.

The instructions below yield an 84" x 68" spread, ideal for a twin bed with dust ruffle.

INSTRUCTIONS

Motif size

Through rnd 4 = 1½" diameter
Through rnd 7 = 3" diameter

You need

- 27 balls #20 cotton crochet thread, 400 yds. each
- Size 10 steel crochet hook

To make large motifs

Make 357.

1st motif

Forming ring. Ch 8, join with sl st to 1st ch.
Rnd 1. Ch 5, *1 dc in ring, ch 2* 11 times, join
with sl st in 3rd ch of ch 5. This forms 12
spokes.

Rnd 2. Work 3 sc in 1st sp between spokes;
repeat, working 3 sc in each sp around,
forming a rnd of 36 sts. Join with sl st under
top 2 threads of 1st sc.

Rnd 3. (This rnd is made of 12 clusters; each
cluster has 4 spokes. The 1st spoke of the 1st
cluster is a ch. For each cluster, work 4
spokes in each group of 3 sc.) 1st cluster: Ch
4, *yo twice, insert hook in joining, yo, draw
through, yo, draw through 2 loops on hook,
yo; draw through 2 more loops* 3 times (4
loops on hook for 1st cluster of rnd, 5 for all
following clusters) working in consecutive
sc's. To complete 1st cluster, yo and draw
through all loops on hook. Ch 4. Work 11
more clusters as 1st. Separate clusters with ch
4. Join last ch to top of 1st cluster with sl st.

Rnd 4. 1st spoke of 1st cluster: sc in ch 4 sp,
ch 4. Proceed making 12 clusters as in rnd 3,
except into sps; ch 8 after each cluster. Join
last ch to top of 1st cluster with sl st.

Rnd 5. *Sc 8 in ch 8 sp, 1 sc in center of next
cluster* around. Join last sc to 1st with sl st.

Rnds 6 and 7. Work 1 sc in each sc around.

Rnd 8. *Ch 8, skip 4 sc, sc in next sc* around,
ending with sc in base of 1st ch 8.

Rnd 9. *Ch 8, 1 sc in 1st ch 8 of rnd 8, ch 8, 1
sc in next ch 8 sp* around, ending with 1 sc in
1st ch 8 sp of rnd 9, ch 8, 1 sc in next ch 8 sp,
fasten off.

2nd large motif

Work as 1st motif through rnd 8. Work rnd 9
as 1st motif through the sc in the last ch 8 sp
of rnd 8.

Joining 1st and 2nd motifs. Ch 4, sc 1 in ch 8
sp of rnd 9 on 1st motif; ch 4, sc 1 in 1st ch 8
sp of rnd 9 on 2nd motif; ch 4, sc 1 in next ch
8 sp of 1st motif; ch 4, sc 1 in next ch 8 sp on
2nd motif, fasten off.

3rd large motif

Work as 2nd motif.

Joining 3rd motif. Sk 10 ch 8 sps from joining
of 1st and 2nd motifs; work joining as above.

Continue making and joining motifs until 21
motifs are joined in a row.

1st motif on row 2

Work as previous motifs through rnd 8. Work
rnd 9 through the 18th sc in ch 8 sp, ch 4, sk 4
ch 8 sps from where the last 2 motifs were
joined in the 1st row, join in the next 2 ch 8 sps
as before, complete this motif as previous
motifs, fasten off.

2nd motif on row 2

Work as 1st motif on row 2 to the sc in the
18th ch 8 sp, sk 5 ch 8 sps on the 20th motif
of the last row, where it joined to the 21st
motif, make joining in 6th and 5th ch 8 sps.
Work around motif and join it to the 1st motif
of this row, fasten off.

Continue making and joining motifs until there
are 21 motifs in 2nd row. Work 15 more rows.

To make small motifs

Make 320.

Work rnds 1-3 as in large motif.

Rnd 4. *Sc 5 in next ch 4 sp, sc 3 in center of
cluster, sc 5 in next ch 4 sp, sc 1 in center of
next cluster.

Joining to 4 large motifs. Join small motifs to
center 2 ch 8 sps. Sk 1 ch 8 sp on a large
motif, sc in next ch 8 sp, sc 1 back in the
center of the same small-motif cluster, sc 5 in
next ch 4 sp, sc 1 in center of next cluster, sc 1
in next ch 8 sp of large motif, sc 1 back in
center of same small motif cluster* 4 times,
once on each of 4 large motifs.

Continue making and joining small motifs
until 320 are joined.

Mr. & Mrs. Robert White
2415 Brandywine Lane
Sudbury, Mass. 01776

Ms. Gretchen McCarthy
25 Forestview Drive
Chicago, Il 60611

Mr. & Mrs. James Adams
15 River Street
Pittsburgh, Pa. 15217

Block Printing

Here's a simple yet striking method of duplicating any design many times over. Use our bird designs on holiday greetings, personal stationery, gift tags and many other pieces—or create and block print a design that's uniquely your own. For variety, print different items with different shades of ink ranging from primary to pastel.

Draw a picture on a linoleum block, carve around the pattern, coat the raised surface with ink, then press block and paper together. With patience and care, the results will be clear, bold and bright—no matter how many copies you make. All the tools you need for block printing are available at art-supply stores. Remember that the design you cut on the block will be reversed when printed.

INSTRUCTIONS

You need

- Block Printing Patterns (page 186)
- Artist's tracing paper
- Soft (#1) lead pencil
- Sandpaper block
- Four 3" x 4" linoleum blocks
- Masking tape
- Artist's knife
- Linoleum cutter and blades
- Block-printing oil-base inks in desired colors
- Piece of glass with edges taped
- Palette knife
- Brayer
- Notepaper and envelopes in desired colors
- Spoon or baren
- Poster board (optional)

To make

1. With tracing paper and pencil, trace desired bird design from Block Printing Patterns. When tracing is complete, rub side of pencil point over outline to create "carbon paper"; with sandpaper block, keep pencil point sharp during rubbing.

2. With masking tape, tape tracing paper, carbon side down, on top of linoleum block. Draw pencil over outline firmly. Remove paper and with pencil, darken traced line.

3. With artist's knife, carefully cut around outline (including bird's eye).

4. Place block against solid object, such as a wall, and with U-shaped linoleum-cutting blade, carve away background. Always carve away from yourself to avoid accidents; carve steadily and keep your fingers behind blade. Finished carved surface should be smooth and 1/16" or more below outlined surface.

5. With palette knife, mix inks in desired colors on glass. Roll brayer over inks until they are smooth with no peaks. Apply smooth ink surface to design with a smooth brayer motion. Place paper to be printed face down on top of inked design and burnish with heel of spoon or baren until ink is absorbed by paper. Carefully peel away paper; let dry for several days.

6. Repeat step 5 for each sheet of paper and each envelope to be printed. If desired, cut gift tags to desired size from poster board and repeat step 5.

Calligraphy

Complement your invitations, envelopes, place cards, gift tags or any written announcements with the personal touch of calligraphy — the ancient art of hand lettering in flowing script. You'll find everything you need to begin calligraphy at art-supply stores.

Calligraphy is somewhat of a science, with exact formulas for letter sizes. Begin by using the Tracing Paper Method and our alphabet, then experiment freehand with different pen nibs and letter sizes. Hold the pen at a 45-degree angle to the paper and never exert great pressure while you are lettering. You will soon develop a calligraphic style that's uniquely your own.

INSTRUCTIONS

You need

- Flat work surface
- Pen holder
- 1 or more C (flat round-point) pen nibs
- India ink
- Scrap paper
- Tracing paper
- Soft (#1) lead pencil
- Sandpaper block
- Stationery or gift tags in desired colors
- Kneaded eraser
- Drafting pencil
- Ruler or T square

To make

Fit nib firmly into penholder. Work on flat, firm surface. Dip nib into India ink and draw a few strokes on scrap paper. Hold the pen at a 45° angle to the paper; this angle enables you to form successfully the thick and thin lines characteristic of calligraphy. Do not exert great pressure.

Tracing paper method

Practice. Lay tracing paper over Calligraphy Pattern (see photograph). Dip pen in ink, draw a few strokes on scrap paper to eliminate excess ink, then draw pen over letters, following the arrows that indicate direction of strokes. Practice letters until they flow naturally and comfortably.

Lettering. In pencil trace letters you plan to use on tracing paper, following lines carefully and creating the words and phrases of your choice. With sandpaper block, keep pencil sharp. Turn over the tracing paper and, with the side of your pencil, heavily shade the letters (you're making carbon paper). Now, turn the tracing paper right side up and position it on stationery or tag. Trace over letters with pencil point. The shaded area on the back will reproduce the letters you've traced. Remove tracing paper. Go over the penciled message with pen and ink. When letters are dry, gently erase stray pencil marks.

Freehand method

Practice. With drafting pencil and ruler or T square, draw guidelines on scrap paper; capital letters should be twice as high as lowercase letters. With sandpaper block, keep drafting pencil leads sharp. Practice lettering between the lines. Experiment with different nibs and different spacing between guidelines.

Lettering. Align stationery or gift tags and draw guidelines with drafting pencil or ruler. Complete lettering; let dry. With kneaded eraser, carefully erase pencil lines.

Sing sweet as the flute,
Sing clear as the horn,
Sing Joy of the creatures,
Come Christmas the morn.

a b c d e f g h i j k l m n o
p q r s t u v w x y z

A B C D E F G H I J K L M N
O P Q R S T U V W X Y Z
1 2 3 4 5 6 7 8 9 0 ?!.,""

Embroidered Apron

Traditional embroidery from the island of Crete inspired this design. Influenced by the handwork of both Venetian and Turkish captors, Cretan embroidery is an interesting blend of Western and Eastern motifs. It is usually worked in panels characterized by stylized flowers and the Cretan feather stitch.

After the Greek Revolution of 1820 the traditional embroidery became rare. Mothers sadly separated their elaborate bedspreads into individual panels so that each betrothed daughter could take at least one piece of the fine needlework to her new home.

The embroidery on this apron is worked in four basic stitches with 16 colors of embroidery thread. Cotton thread is good, but for added sheen and a more authentic look, use silk. The apron is made from an easy-care polyester-and-linen-blend fabric.

Stitch the traditional motifs on cushions, guest towels, table linens, curtains, carryalls, blouses, skirts, sleeves and sashes to give brand-new possessions Old World charm.

INSTRUCTIONS

You need

- Embroidered Apron Patterns (pages 187 - 190)
- 1 yd. 60"-wide beige polyester/flax fabric
- Transferring Patterns materials (see page 206)
- Beige thread
- Skeins of cotton or silk embroidery thread as follows:

1 white	1 yellow
5 gold	3 bright blue
2 rose	3 dark blue
3 red	2 gold-brown
2 dark green	2 dark brown
1 medium green	2 beige
1 violet	1 medium brown
1 purple	4 black
1 bright gold	

To cut and embroider fabric

1. Cut fabric into the following pieces, according to layout in Fig. 1:

    2 rectangles for apron bib, 13" x 11" each
    2 rectangles for skirt, 27" x 24" each
    2 waistbands, 13" x 2¾" each
    (1 of each of above pieces is for lining)

2. With Transferring Patterns Materials, transfer Embroidered Apron Pattern 1 to one 13" x 11" rectangle and Pats. 2, 3, 4 and 5 to one 27" x 24" rectangle, following layout in Fig. 2. Draw Pats. 1, 4 and 5 on apron to right side of apron's center, then reverse and draw on left side of apron's center. To reverse design, turn over tracing paper, place carbon paper carbon side down, between tracing paper and fabric, then draw over lines as before (see Fig. 2).

3. Embroider bib and skirt of apron according to stitches and colors given with Pats. 1-5.

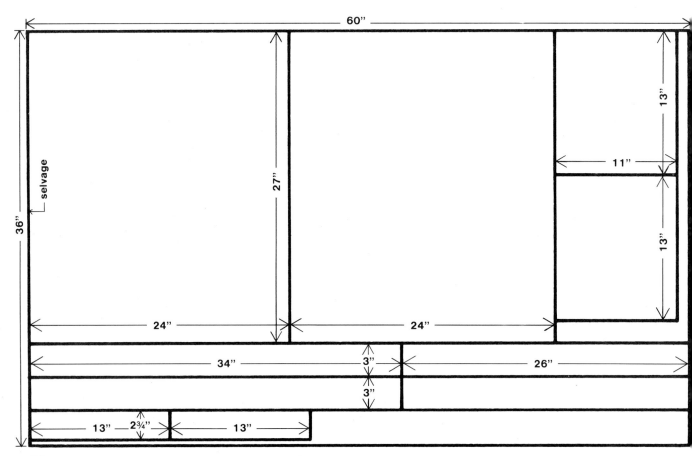

**FIG.1
CUTTING LAYOUT**

To make apron

1. Fold each 26" x 3" shoulder strap in half lengthwise; stitch along 1 short edge and the long open edge in ¼" seam. Turn to right side and press. Pin each shoulder strap to top edge of right side of embroidered bib section, 1⅝" from side edge, matching raw edges. Baste straps to bib in ½" seam.

2. With right sides together, stitch the 2 bib pieces together along the side and top edges in ½" seam. Trim seam allowance to ¼", clip along corners and turn to right side; press.

3. With right sides together, stitch 2 skirt pieces together along side and bottom edges in ½" seam. Trim seam allowance to ¼", clip across corners and turn to right side. To hold lining in place understitch on all 3 seams as follows: On right side of lining, topstitch through lining and both seam allowances close to the seam line. Press. Baste the open edges on bib and on skirt closed in ½" seam. To gather apron skirt, run 2 lines of basting stitches within waistline seam allowance and gather to fit waistband.

4. On 1 waistband piece, turn under ½" seam allowance on all edges; press. Stitch basted edge of bib to 1 long edge of waistband in ½" seam, right sides together. Stitch basted edge of skirt to other long edge of waistband in ½" seam, right sides together.

5. On each 34" x 3" tie, turn under ¼" twice on 1 short and 2 long edges; stitch in place. Stitch remaining cut edge of each tie to short edge of waistband in ½" seam, right sides together. Press wrong side of waistband so all seam allowances are turned toward waistband. Turn under ½" seam allowance on all edges of remaining waistband piece; press. Whipstitch remaining band to wrong side of stitched waistband, matching all edges.

6. Try on apron, tying at waist. Fold ends of shoulder straps to form loops for inserting waistband ties. Adjust for comfortable fit; stitch in place.

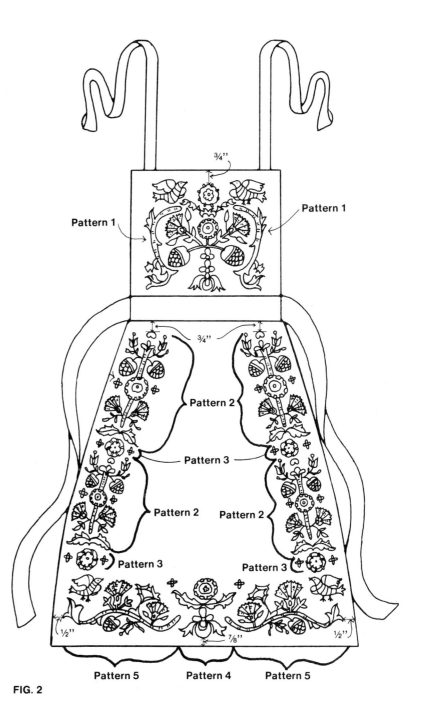

FIG. 2

Sleeping Bag

Here's a sunny sleeping bag perfect for slumber parties or special camp-out days. Machine appliqué decorates the top of the bag, and sturdy cotton/polyester fabrics (scraps from your sewing box?) complete the design. Pad the bag with layers of batting for warmth without weight. At wake-up time, roll up the bag and stash it in a closet. The bag also makes an ideal extra bed for unexpected houseguests.

INSTRUCTIONS

You need

- Sleeping Bag Patterns (page 191)
- 2¼ yds. each green and blue 45"-wide medium-weight cotton/polyester blend fabric
- Brown wrapping paper
- Enlarging Patterns materials (see page 206)
- Scraps and remnants of cotton in colors listed in Pat. 2 or colors of your choice
- Black and green thread
- 4⅝ yds. 45"-wide preshrunk muslin
- 4⅝ yds. 45"-wide medium-weight cotton/polyester blend fabric, for lining
- 2 sheets 81" x 96" each batting or 2 sheets 72" x 96" each extra-lofty batting (pieced if necessary)
- 100" length of self-adhering fastener
- 2 oz. of 4-ply knitting worsted in a variety of colors
- Sharp yarn needle

To make

1. With brown wrapping paper, cut pattern according to Sleeping Bag Pattern 1. Cut exterior back from green fabric and front from blue fabric, allowing 1" seam allowances.

2. With Enlarging Patterns Materials, bring Sleeping Bag Pat. 2 up to full size. Cut each segment of Pat. 2, except blue sky, out of paper. With paper segments, cut appliqué pieces from scraps and remnants of cotton, adding a ½" seam allowance around each piece. Arrange pieces on blue sleeping bag front in the following order: sunrays; cloud and bird; hills; tree trunks; tree leaves; apples. Pin or hand baste in place. With black thread, zigzag around all pieces ½" from edge, stitching lower layer pieces such as hills first. Trim fabric along stitching. Zigzag again to reinforce cut edge. If desired, add extra zigzag lines to clouds. Cut rounded corners in appliqué layer.

3. With right sides together, stitch front and back together along entire length of straight edge in 1" seam. Press seam open.

4. Cut muslin and lining fabric according to Pat. 1. Stitch muslin sections together as in step 3. Stitch lining sections together, leaving a 20" opening at center seam.

5. Padding bag. Pin 2 layers of batting to wrong side of muslin. Trim ¾" from outer edge of batting. Do not trim muslin. Baste batting to muslin close to edge.

6. With batting to wrong side of bag, pin muslin section to bag. Outer edges of muslin and bag should be even. Machine baste ⅝" from edge all around.

7. With right sides together, pin and stitch lining to bag all around edge in ⅞" seam. Turn to right side through lining opening; whipstitch opening closed.

8. Quilting bag. Stitch yarn ties at 6" to 7" intervals over entire bag as follows: Thread a sharp yarn needle with yarn. Push needle through all thicknesses of bag from right side to wrong side and back to right side about ¼" away. Tie ends of yarn in a square knot and clip yarn to 1".

Child's Sweater

Jelly-bean colors flavor this pullover that perks up any child on a gray winter day. Choose an easy-care Orlon or a wool yarn in one of the heavier weights. The front-side zipper closing makes it a simple sweater to pull on and off—a must for children, who don't like to let winter slow them down! We added a purchased hat for a candy-bright twosome.

INSTRUCTIONS

Sizes

Instructions are for children's size 6 with changes for sizes 8, 10 and 12 in (   ).

Gauge

5 sts = 1"
6 rows = 1"

You need

- 4-ply Orlon or wool knitting worsted as follows:
     2 (3, 3, 4) oz. each bright blue, orange and red
     2 oz. each purple and green
     1 oz. tangerine
- No. 5 knitting needles
- No. 8 knitting needles
- 3 stitch holders
- Blunt yarn needle
- 6" purple neckline zipper
- Purple thread
- Sewing needle

To make

When changing colors, always twist one color around the other (on wrong side of work) to prevent making holes.

Starting at neck edge with tangerine and no. 5 needles, co 73 (79, 79, 83) sts. Work in k 1, p 1 ribbing for 1", dec 1 st in center of last row—72 (78, 78, 82) sts. Change to no. 8 needles. Next row: Drop tangerine, attach red, p 12 (13, 13, 14), drop red, attach orange, p 12 (13, 13, 14) for Front; place marker on needle. Drop orange, attach green p 12 (13, 13, 13) for Sleeve; place marker on needle. Drop green, attach blue, p 24 (26, 26, 28) for Back; place marker on needle. Drop blue, attach purple, p 12 (13, 13, 13) for Sleeve.

Continuing in established colors, work in st st as follows: Row 1 (right side): *K in front and back of next st—an inc is made; k across to within 2 sts before next marker, inc in next st as before, k 1, slip marker* 3 times; inc in next st, k across to within last 2 sts, inc in next st, k 1—8 sts increased. Row 2: Slipping markers, p across. Repeat Rows 1 and 2 alternately until there are 44 (49, 51, 53) sts on each Sleeve and 56 (62, 64, 68) sts on Front and Back, ending with a p row. Next row: K to next marker, sl marker, inc in next st, k across to within 2 sts before next marker, inc in next st, k 1, sl marker, k across to next marker, sl marker, inc in next st, k across to within last 2 sts, inc in next st, k 1—4 sts increased (no inc on Sleeves). Next row: Slipping markers, p across. Repeat last 2 rows 1 more time—60 (66, 68, 72) sts on Front and Back; 44 (49, 51, 53) sts on each Sleeve. Break off yarns. Removing markers, slip sts of 1 Sleeve, Back and Front onto separate stitch holders to be worked later.

Sleeve

Co 3 sts on the free no. 8 needle for underarm. With right side facing, k across sleeve sts on needle; co 3 at end of row for other underarm—50 (55, 57, 59) sts. Continue in st st, dec 1 st at both ends of every 8th (9th, 8th, 9th) row 6 (7, 8, 8) times in all. Work even on 38 (41, 41, 43) sts until length from underarm is 10" (11½", 12½", 14½"), ending with a p row and dec 4 (5, 5, 5) sts evenly spaced across last row. Change to no. 5 needles and tangerine, work in k 1, p 1 ribbing over remaining 34 (36, 36, 38) sts for 1½". Bind off loosely in ribbing. Sl the sts of other Sleeve onto a no. 8 needle and work same as 1st Sleeve.

Back

Slip sts of Back onto a no. 8 needle. Co 3 sts on free no. 8 needle for underarm; with right side facing, k across back sts; co 3 sts at end of row for other underarm. Work even in st st over 66 (72, 74, 78) sts until length of underarm is 7″ (7½″, 8½″, 9½″), ending with a p row and dec 2 sts in each row. Change to no. 5 needles and tangerine; work in k 1, p 1 ribbing for 1½″ (1½″, 2″, 2″). Bind off loosely in ribbing.

Front

Sl rem 60 (66, 68, 72) sts onto a no. 8 needle and, matching colors, complete as for Back.

Finishing

Block pieces if desired. Sew side, sleeve and underarm seams with yarn. With thread, stitch zipper in opening between Left Sleeve and Front. If necessary, stitch Sleeve to Front below zipper.

Puffy Quilt

Stitch and stuff a group of favorite prints to make a quilt that's also a blanket or bedspread. It's puffy because it's made in 64 small squares, each filled with lightweight polyester fiber stuffing. And the quilt's softness and warmth — without excess weight — will be welcome on cold winter nights.

INSTRUCTIONS

You need

- Four 54"-wide print fabrics as follows:
    1¾ yds. pattern 1
    1½ yds. each patterns 2, 3 and 4
- 7 yds. 36"-wide unbleached muslin
- 5¼ yds. 45"-wide solid-color fabric
- Thread to match solid color
- 11 lbs. polyester fiber stuffing

To make

1. Cut print fabrics in sixty-four 12½" squares as follows:

Pattern 1: 19 squares
Pattern 2: 16 squares
Pattern 3: 15 squares
Pattern 4: 14 squares

2. Cut muslin into sixty-four 11" squares. Cut a 3" slash in center of each muslin square (Fig. 1).

3. Lay muslin squares on floor to form a large square with 8 muslin squares on a side. Arrange print squares by pattern number on muslin squares (Fig. 2). Pin each print square to a muslin square, taking 2 small equal pleats 4" apart on each side of print square so all edges match (Fig. 3). Finger-press pleats toward center of each side. Stitch print square to muslin ½" from edge. Repeat pinning and stitching with each square, working 1 row at a time.

4. Assembling quilt top. Stitch squares in Row A together end to end, right sides together, with ½" seam allowance. Repeat with each row. Stitch rows together in same way. Completed quilt top should measure about 81" x 81".

5. Cut backing fabric in half for two 94½" x 45" pieces. With right sides together, stitch halves in ½" seam allowance along one long edge. Press seam open; press backing flat. Backing should measure 89" x 94½".

6. Place backing on floor, wrong side up. Place top over backing, right side up, centering top so a 4" border of backing shows along all edges. Trim away any backing in excess of 4" border. Baste top to backing ½" from edge, leaving 60" opening along 1 edge for turning. On backing, fold ½" to wrong side on all edges; press. Fold border in half so pressed fold meets basting; press. At corners, fold 1 border in first; then fold other border over 1st at right angles. Topstitch close to border fold through all thicknesses. Whipstitch corner folds in place. Remove basting stitches.

7. Turn quilt to wrong side. Separate a 1-lb. bag of polyester fiber stuffing into 6 equal parts and stuff 6 squares through slashes in muslin. Whipstitch each slash closed by hand. Repeat with all squares. Turn quilt to right side through opening. Finish border at opening (step 6).

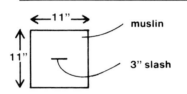

FIG.1
MUSLIN SQUARE

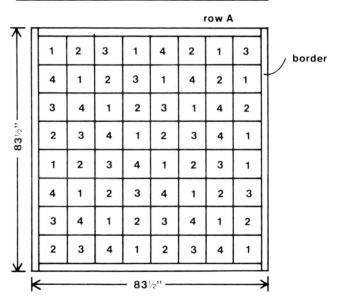

FIG.2
PRINT-SQUARE PLACEMENT

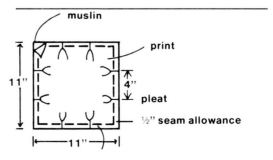

FIG.3
STITCHING SQUARES

Acrylic Desk Set

Clear acrylic plastic in sheets and pieces and easy-to-use tools create home and office accessories that offer a clean, uncluttered look. They're easy to clean and go well with almost any decor.

The General Acrylic Instructions (page 192) explain the basic techniques of working with acrylic plastic. Refer to them as you make the picture frame, letter tray, pen stand, desk calendar or note box. Be sure to cut and sand the pieces of acrylic so that they fit together exactly when bonded. Salespeople at your hardware store or plastics-supply house can assist you in obtaining the exact tools you need to make these beautiful desk accessories.

Refer to General Acrylic Instructions (page 192) before beginning and while working.

PICTURE FRAME INSTRUCTIONS

You need

- $\frac{3}{16}$" acrylic sheet 21" x 20"
- Scribe-and-break cutting materials
- 4 screw fasteners
- Drill bit same size as fasteners
- Drilling materials
- Sanding and polishing materials
- Bonding materials

To make

1. Cut two 7" x 9" pieces and 1 right triangle with 7" and 2" sides for right angle from acrylic sheet.

2. On one 7" x 9" piece, mark a point at each corner exactly ¾" from sides. Drill holes at these 4 points. Place drilled piece atop other 7" x 9" piece; match edges and mark positions of holes on bottom piece. Drill holes as above.

3. Sand and polish 7" and 2" edges of triangle and all 4 edges on each 7" x 9" piece. Sand but do not polish remaining triangle edge.

4. Place one 7" x 9" piece on work surface. Place triangle on top with longest edge down. Position so triangle is in center of frame with point toward top, and bottom of triangle is at bottom edge of frame. Hold in place and apply a small amount of solvent at 1 end of seam. If solvent does not flow full length of seam, apply a bit more where needed. Apply slight pressure for a few seconds; let stand 5 minutes.

5. Place picture between layers of frame and fasten at holes with screw fasteners.

PICTURE FRAME

LETTER TRAY INSTRUCTIONS

You need

- ³⁄₁₆" acrylic sheet 47⅝" x 35⅝"
- Scribe-and-break cutting materials
- Sanding and polishing materials
- Grease pencil (optional)
- Coping saw (optional)
- Masking tape
- Bonding materials

To make

1. Cut one 10" x 12" for base, two 2" x 11⅝" for sides and two 2" x 10" pieces for ends from acrylic sheet. If desired, with grease pencil mark curve 5" long and ⅝" deep at deepest point in center of long edge of one 2" x 10" piece. Cut with coping saw.

2. Sand and polish the following: 1 long and 2 short edges (including curved edge) of two 2" x 10" end pieces; 1 long edge of each of two 2" x 11⅝" side pieces; all 4 edges of 10" x 12" base. Sand but do not polish all remaining edges.

3. Place base on work surface. Place end and side pieces, polished edges up, on top of base along edges. Tape box together, precisely matching edges and corners. Bond pieces to base by applying small amount of solvent at each corner. If solvent does not flow full length of seam, apply a bit more where needed. Apply slight pressure to top edges for a few seconds. Let set 5 minutes. Stand box on 1 end and with same procedure, bond corner seams. Repeat with other end.

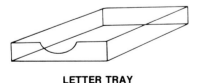

LETTER TRAY

PEN STAND INSTRUCTIONS

You need

- ³⁄₁₆" acrylic sheet 16" x 16"
- Scribe-and-break cutting materials
- ¼" acrylic drill bit
- Drilling materials
- ¼" x ¾" acrylic peg
- Bonding materials
- 2" length of hollow acrylic tube
- Saw
- 2 books or pieces of plywood of equal thickness
- 1 purchased desk-set pen

To make

1 Cut one 4⅜" x 6½" piece, one 3½" x 5½" piece, one 2¾" x 4¾" piece and one 1¼" x 3" piece from acrylic sheet.

2. With pencil and ruler, draw a diagonal line on protective paper from corner to corner on each piece. Draw a 2nd diagonal line connecting other corners. Drill a hole in center of each piece, placing point of bit precisely at intersection of lines.

3. Check fit. Stack pieces with largest on bottom and smallest on top. Line up holes and be sure edges run parallel to each other. Slide acrylic peg into hole; fit should be snug but not forced and peg should line up with top and bottom of stack. Remove peg, unstack pieces. Sand peg or holes if needed. Sand and polish all 4 edges of each piece. Re-stack pieces to check fit; remove top 3 pieces, leaving peg inserted in bottom piece.

4. On work surface place 2 books or pieces of plywood parallel to each other 4½" apart. Place largest piece (with peg) atop books so peg is in center of space between books. Bottom of peg should be even with bottom of rectangle. With applicator, apply 1 drop of solvent to seam where peg and rectangle meet. Let set 5 minutes; check bond. If peg turns in hole, apply more solvent. Slide next rectangle on peg; position so edges are parallel and bond as above. Continue until all 4 pieces are stacked and bonded, allowing 5 minutes for setting each time.

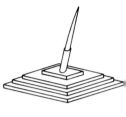

PEN STAND

5. Angle the end of hollow acrylic tube by cutting with saw. Sand with #150 sandpaper. Sand and polish blunt end of tube. Check fit by positioning angled end over peg so tube leans toward 1 edge of stack. Remove tube, apply small amount of solvent around peg, place angled end of tube on solvent ring, apply slight pressure and hold in place 30-60 seconds. Let set 5 minutes. Place purchased pen in tube.

DESK CALENDAR INSTRUCTIONS

You need

- ³⁄₁₆" acrylic sheet 14" x 7½"
- Scribe-and-break cutting materials
- 1 purchased 5" x 8" calendar pad with holes at top edge
- Pencil
- Acrylic drill bit
- Drilling materials
- Two ½" acrylic balls
- 2 screws
- Plastic cement or any glue that dries clear and hard
- Scrap of felt

To make

1. Cut one 5½" x 8" and one 5½" x 2" piece from acrylic sheet. Center 1 sheet of calendar pad on larger acrylic piece. With pencil, mark positions of 2 holes on protective paper; drill holes. Using larger piece as a guide, mark positions of holes on smaller piece. Drill as above.

2. Drill a hole about halfway into each acrylic ball. Sand and polish all edges of acrylic pieces. Place screws in holes in larger acrylic piece; stack calendar pad and then smaller piece of acrylic on top so threaded ends of screw protrude from calendar. Hold ball with hole facing up; apply a few drops plastic cement in hole. Invert assembled calendar and

insert threaded end of screw into ball. Let cement set according to manufacturer's instructions. Repeat with other ball.

3. Cut 2 small circles of felt to fit heads of screws. Glue felt to screws.

NOTE BOX INSTRUCTIONS

You need

- ³⁄₁₆" acrylic sheet 11½" x 30¾"
- Scribe-and-break cutting materials
- Grease pencil (optional)
- Coping saw (optional)
- Masking tape
- Bonding materials
- Purchased 4" x 6" pad of paper

To make

1. Cut two 1¼" x 5⅞" pieces for sides, two 1¼" x 4¼" pieces for end, one 4¼" x 6¼" piece for base and one 2¼" x 4¼" piece for top from acrylic sheet. If desired, with grease pencil mark curve 2⅝" long and ½" deep at deepest point in center of long edge of one 1¼" x 4¼" end piece; cut with coping saw.

2. Assemble following Letter Tray Instructions, steps 2 and 3.

3. Place rectangular top piece over 1 end of open box, matching edges to check fit. Remove top. Apply a small amount of solvent to 3 edges of box where top was positioned; replace top with edges matching; apply slight pressure and hold 30 seconds. Let set 5 minutes. Fill box with purchased paper.

NOTE BOX

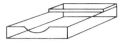

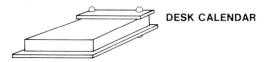

DESK CALENDAR

Children's
Backpack

A backpack is the ideal way for children to tote everything they need for schooltime and playtime. Cut out the pieces for this one in plain canvas; then let your child decorate it with original pictures, designs or lettering. Ball-point indelible-ink markers (available in art-supply stores) make decorating easy and colors won't fade in the washing machine. Flags, ships, trees, flowers, racing cars, animals or just doodles — let your child's imagination take its own course.

When decorating is complete, stitch the backpack together. Then topstitch straps, closures and trim, all of heavy-duty tape, to the canvas.

INSTRUCTIONS

You need

- Backpack Pattern (page 193)
- Enlarging Patterns materials (see page 206)
- ½ yd. 45"-wide heavy-duty canvas or duck fabric
- 5 yds. 1"-wide twill or heavy-duty tape
- 4 semicircular belt rings, 1⅛" diameter
- Heavy-duty thread
- Ball-point embroidery paint markers in a variety of colors

To make

1. With Enlarging Patterns Materials, bring Backpack Pattern up to full size. Cut 1 each front, back, side and flap section from fabric. Cut tape into 10 lengths as follows: two 7", two 10", two 12", two 22", one 21" and one 29". Decorate backpack pieces as desired with markers before stitching.

2. Closing straps. Topstitch the 10" tapes to front section in X-in-square pattern shown in Pattern, turning under cut edge. Turn under and stitch remaining cut edge on each strap. With right sides together, stitch 3-sided curved edge of front section to 1 long edge of side panel in ⅜" seam. Press seam allowance toward side panel; topstitch through seam allowance on side panel ¼" from seam.

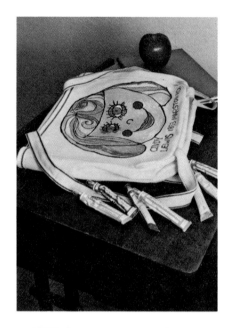

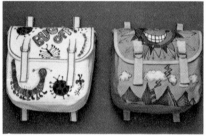

3. Bind upper edge of side-front piece with 21" tape: fold tape in half over edge and top-stitch in place through all thicknesses. Bind straight edge of back section in same manner with 12" tape. Bind portion of flap section edge indicated by dotted line in Pattern with 29" tape.

4. Sling straps. Topstitch 22" tapes to right side of flap section (see Pattern). Topstitch 12" piece of tape across flap section, covering stitched ends of arm sling straps (see Pattern).

5. Place back section on flap section so wrong side of back and right side of flap face each other; back will become backpack pocket. Stitch 3-sided curved edge in ⅜" seam, keeping sling straps free of stitching. Pin ends of sling straps to seam in position indicated in Pattern. Baste straps along seam line. With right sides together, pin back to long un-stitched edge of side panel; stitch in ⅜" seam and press seam allowance toward side panel. Turn to right side; topstitch seam allowance on side panel ¼" from seam.

6. Belt ring straps. Fold 7" tapes in half to form double thickness of tape. Slip 2 belt rings on each double thickness of tape. Fold lengths in half again so belt rings are enclosed in loop; topstitch ends to flap section in position indicated in Pattern, placing folded end of strap on top of cut end.

7. If finishing touches are needed, complete decorating backpack with ball-point embroidery paint markers in desired design. ○

Fabric Painting

It isn't dyeing, it's painting with dyes—in swirls and dips and flowing lines on any fabric or garment that's made of natural fibers (synthetics won't hold the dyes). Procion dyes have superior colorfastness, but they are toxic, so keep a separate set of utensils for your fabric-painting work. Use only porcelain, glass or enamel containers, too. Always wash fabrics before painting; painted garments can be dry cleaned or washed by hand.

Gauge your designs according to the weight and dimensions of your fabric. Use broader brush strokes and bolder color areas on larger and heavier pieces, smaller strokes on delicate items like scarves. If you are working with finished garments, pin garment directly onto work surface or over a cardboard cutout, depending on the type of garment. The borders of our kimono were pinned directly on the work surface and painted, while the shoulders were painted over cardboard cutouts.

INSTRUCTIONS

You need

- 4' x 8' sheet ½" interior insulation board, white face
- 5' x 9' sheet carpet padding or several layers polyester batting
- 5' x 9' plastic drop cloth
- 5' x 9' piece of unbleached muslin
- Staples and staple gun
- Old sheet
- Large and small screw-top jars
- Measuring spoons
- 1 teaspoon calgonite
- 10 tablespoons urea
- 2 cups hot water
- 2 cups cold water
- 3 teaspoons sodium alginate
- Mixing bowl
- Electric hand mixer and beaters
- Procion powder dyes in desired colors
- Mixing spoons
- 2 tablespoons baking soda
- Double-pointed jewelry pins or T-pins
- Natural-fiber fabric
- Cardboard (optional)
- Artist's paintbrushes
- Steam iron (optional)

To prepare work surface

Lay sheet of insulation board over table. Cover with padding, drop cloth and muslin in that order. Pull coverings around to back of insulation board and staple in place, stretching coverings for taut fit. Cover muslin with sheet and staple in place.

To mix dyes

1. Chemical water. In large screw-top jar, dissolve 1 teaspoon calgonite and 10 tablespoons urea in 2 cups hot water by shaking. Add 2 cups cold water and shake. (To mix black or gray dyes use 3 tablespoons urea per quart of water.)

2. Pour chemical water into mixing bowl. Sprinkle 3 teaspoons sodium alginate over it. Beat with electric hand mixer for about 5 minutes. Let paste stand 30 minutes, or pour into screw-top jar, cap tightly and let stand overnight. (Dye paste will keep for 2 weeks if capped tightly.)

3. Mixing. To mix pale shades, use ½ teaspoon procion dye; to mix medium shades, use ½-1 teaspoon dye; to mix dark shades, use 1-2 teaspoons or more. Place dye in desired color in jar; to combine 2 or more colors, mix dyes together in jar. Add ½ cup paste by teaspoonfuls at first to assure smooth thick consistency. (Dyes may be stored up to 1 week.)

4. Mix 2 tablespoons baking soda and a few drops tap water; consistency should resemble moist sugar. Add ¼ to ½ teaspoon of baking-soda mixture to each dye; add ¾ to 1½ teaspoons baking-soda mixture to turquoise and black dyes. (Dyes may be stored only 2-3 days; only add soda to amount of dye you think you will use.)

To paint design

1. Pin fabric or garment to work surface or over cardboard cutout, stretching as taut as possible. With dyes in desired colors and artist's paintbrushes, paint design on stretched fabric. Let dry. Remove from work surface and line dry for 24 hours or more. Do not pin additional fabric over work surface where dye has been absorbed by sheet; work on clean areas of work surface. When you can no longer work on a clean area, remove sheet; then wash, bleach and reapply to work surface.

2. Setting dyes. With 1 of these methods, set dyes: with steam iron, press for 5 minutes; air dry in warm, humid place for at least 7 days; hang in steamy bathroom for 1 hour.

3. Rinse fabric or garment in cold running water until water runs clear. Continue to rinse, increasing temperature of water until it feels hot to the touch and water runs clear. Line dry fabric. ○

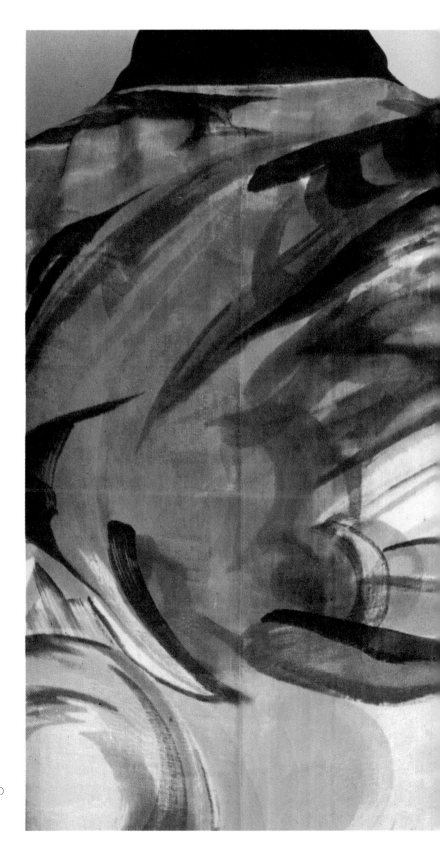

Terrarium

The idea of raising a tiny garden in a closed container began in the 19th century with a Londoner named Dr. Nathanial Ward. He found that the moisture that all green plants emit from their leaves (a process called transpiration) would condense on the walls of a closed container and "rain" down on the plants to be reabsorbed. His discovery led to a Victorian-era craze for "Wardian cases," as terrariums were then known. Many of the Victorian bell jars found today in antique shops started life as Wardian cases.

Choose a clear glass bottle for your terrarium and be sure it is sparkling clean. If your terrarium becomes infested with pests, you will have to clean it completely and start again. Spoon or funnel in gravel and a good soil mixture carefully.

Be sure to select plants with similar light and moisture requirements for each terrarium you make. Ask at the plant store about plants grown especially for terrariums. Limit the number and size of the plants you choose to give each one some growing room. Decide on the placement of plants within the bottle, then carefully place the plants one by one in the container (this takes patience). Be sure to be gentle when you move the finished terrarium from place to place.

Water the terrarium sparingly to begin with, then check it about once a week—though it may not need more water for up to three months. If one plant threatens to crowd out the others, prune the plant with an artist's knife or a sharp blade taped to a dowel.

TERRARIUM PLANTS

These are some of the miniature plants that like the high humidity of a terrarium.

Adiantum species — maidenhair fern; dark green fronds

Alternanthera versicolor — pink, green and white wrinkled foliage

Begonia species

Billbergia nutans — a tropical bromeliad

Caladium — variegated leaves

Calathea species

Cissus striata — miniature grape ivy

Dionea muscipula — Venus fly trap

Dracaena species — striped or spotted leaves for accent

Fittonia species — mosaic plant; white-or pink-veined leaves

Hedera helix — crinkle ivy

Helxine soleirolii — baby's tears; creeper

Maranta species — prayer plant; spotted leaves fold up at night

Pelargonium species — miniature geranium

Pellaca roundifolia — button fern; blue-green foliage

Peperomia species — low-lying; crinkled or spotted leaves

Philodendron — miniature

Pilea micorphylla — artillery plant, low-lying with bright green leaves

Polystichum tsus-simense — dwarf fern; delicate and lacy

Pteris ensiformis victoriae — delicate, light green fern

Saintpaulia species — African violet miniatures

Selaginella species — creepers; foolproof in a closed garden

Tradescantia multiflora — inch plant; creeping, dark-green foliage; must be pruned

INSTRUCTIONS

You need
- Clear glass bottle
- Lintless cloth
- Plants
- Artist's knife or single-edged razor blade taped on dowel
- Small funnel (purchased or made of aluminum foil)
- Clean gravel or aquarium rocks to make 1" layer in container
- Charcoal granules to make ¼" layer in container
- Grabber (24" flexible pick-up tool with retractable claw operated by plunger)
- 2 wooden sticks
- 1 bottlecap
- Basting tube
- Artist's long sable brush
- Coat hanger
- Cotton balls
- Ground cover (optional)
- Decorative rocks, shells or bark (optional)

To make

1. Wash bottle and with lintless cloth, get it sparkling clean inside and outside. Let bottle dry.

2. For a large bottle, cut a newspaper circle of the same diameter as bottle and plan plant placement on it (Fig. 1). Examine plants and with knife, trim bad foliage.

3. Funnel in enough gravel to cover bottle bottom evenly about 1" deep (Fig. 2). Sprinkle ¼" layer of charcoal granules over gravel.

4. Funnel in 3"-5" of very dry soil (amount depends on size of bottle). Tape bottlecap to end of 1 stick to make tamper. With tamper, mound soil in the back if terrarium will be seen from 1 side only; otherwise in the center.

5. With stick, make a hole about 1" deep in the soil near the edge for 1st plant. Tap plant out of pot, gently knock most of the soil off the roots and moisten roots under water tap so they are compact (keep leaves dry).

6. Lower plant through bottleneck, gently compressing the leaves and tipping the bottle if necessary to aim plant at 1" hole. If stems are not too tender, use grabber to lower plant. (See Figs. 3 and 4.) Repeat steps 5 and 6 for each plant, with taller ones or those near the center last.

7. With grabber, hold each plant upright. With tamper, slowly and gently tamp soil around roots, first on one side, then the other, eliminating air pockets.

8. With baster, give each plant about 1 tablespoon water. Do not over-water. Aim baster when watering or use sable brush held with grabber to clean soil from leaves. Attach cotton ball to coat hanger; wipe dirt from sides of bottle.

9. Add ground cover and decorative objects, if desired. Cover terrarium and place in semi-shade for 1 week, then set in location according to light needed by plants.

FIG. 1
Arrange plants on newspaper pattern

FIG. 2
Pour gravel through funnel

FIG. 3
Lower plant into hole with "grabber" or . . .

FIG. 4
. . . drop plant into hole, tipping bottle

FIG. 5
Water sparingly with baster

Felt Games

The game's the thing and half the fun is in the making. These three easy-to-make games-in-the-round are made entirely of felt with iron-on fusing web and a bit of simple machine stitchery. Each game is its own storage bag, too—just put the playing pieces in the circle's center, pull the drawstring ribbon to close the bag, and tie the bag shut. Leave the ribbon in or take it out while playing.

INSTRUCTIONS
Letters in ( ) denote color code in Figures.

Checkers

You need
- Felt as follows:
    - ¾ yd. light orange (shading)
    - ⅛ yd. dark orange (O)
    - ⅛ yd. medium blue (MB)
    - ⅛ yd. dark blue (B)
- 2 yds. iron-on fusing web
- Orange thread
- 2 yds. ⅜" wide orange grosgrain ribbon
- Sixteen 2" styrofoam cubes

Tic-Tac-Toe

You need
- Felt as follows:
    - ¾ yd. green (G)
    - ⅛ yd. dark blue (B)
    - ¼ yd. red (R)
- 1 yd. iron-on fusing web
- Green and red thread
- 2 yds. ⅜" wide blue grosgrain ribbon
- ½ bag polyester fiber stuffing

Backgammon

You need
- Felt as follows:
    - ¾ yd. gold (Gd)
    - ⅛ yd. dark blue (B)
    - ¼ yd. green (G)
    - ¼ yd. turquoise (T)
    - Scraps of white, light and dark orange
- 2 yds. iron-on fusing web
- 5 yds. each ⅜" wide green and turquoise grosgrain ribbon
- Green thread
- 3 yds. ⅜" wide gold grosgrain ribbon

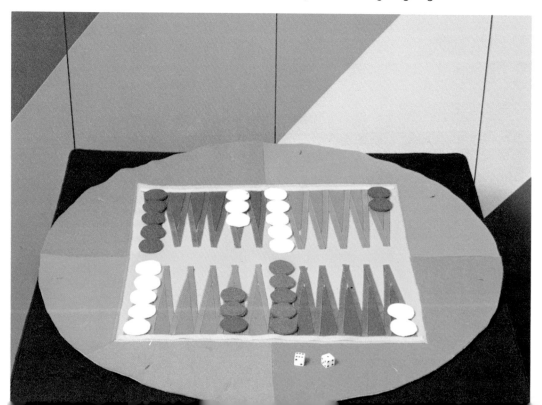

To make game circles

Cut felt into 26"-diameter circles and pieces according to Figs. 1, 2 or 3. Fuse felt pieces in place on circles following iron-on fusing web instructions. Fuse ribbon trim to backgammon circle. Zigzag stitch where indicated in Figures. Space twenty-four ½" machine-stitched buttonholes evenly around each circle, ¾" from edge.

To make checker cubes

Cut sixteen 2" x 6" dark orange felt strips and sixteen 2" x 6" dark blue strips. Fuse felt to styrofoam cubes as in Fig. 1A.

To make Tic-Tac-Toe Pieces

Cut 10 Xs from green felt and 10 Os from red felt as in Fig. 2A. Zigzag together in pairs around edges, wrong sides together, leaving a 2" opening. Stuff with polyester fiber and zigzag opening closed.

To make Backgammon Pieces

Cut thirty 1¼"-diameter circles from white felt and 15 each from light and dark orange. Fuse white circles together in pairs and light and dark orange circles together in pairs (light/light and dark/dark) to make 30 pieces in all.

**FIG. 1
CHECKERS
GAME CIRCLE**

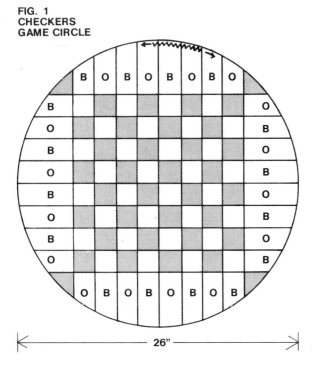

each square = 2" per side

shading denotes light orange background felt

background circle = light orange

all blank squares = MB

⋎⋎⋎⋎⋎ = zigzag stitching

**FIG. 1A
CHECKER CUBES**

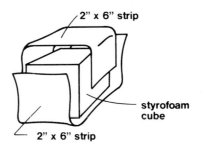

2" x 6" strip

styrofoam cube

2" x 6" strip

26"

FIG. 2
TIC-TAC-TOE
GAME CIRCLE

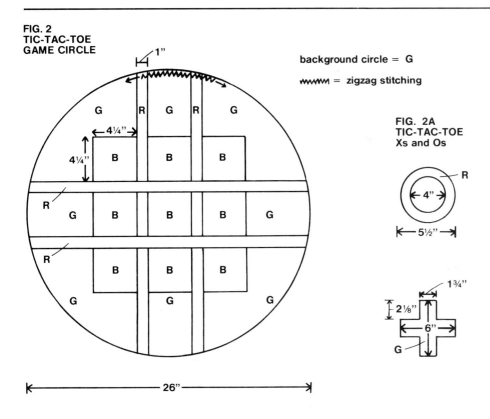

1"

background circle = G

wwwww = zigzag stitching

4¼"

4¼"

G R G R G

B B B

R

G B B B G

R

B B B

G G G

26"

FIG. 2A
TIC-TAC-TOE
Xs and Os

R

4"

5½"

1¾"

2⅛"

6"

G

FIG. 3
BACKGAMMON
GAME CIRCLE

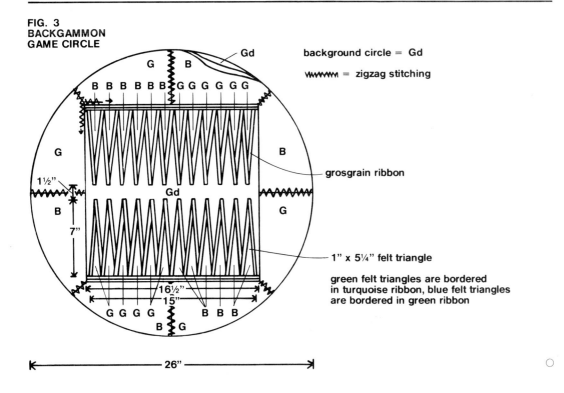

Gd

background circle = Gd

wwwww = zigzag stitching

G B

B B B B B B G G G G G G

G

B

grosgrain ribbon

1½"

Gd

B

G

7"

1" x 5¼" felt triangle

16½"

15"

G G G G B B B

B G

green felt triangles are bordered
in turquoise ribbon, blue felt triangles
are bordered in green ribbon

26"

Bookbinding

The medieval craft of bookbinding requires just a few simple tools and some special care. Supplies you don't already have at home are readily available in art-supply shops. Bind up a few dreams, a thought or poem, favorite photos or baby's first words. Collect vacation mementos or carry a book with blank pages for last-minute reminder notes. Make a book of recipes as a bridal gift. Books you bind yourself have so many uses. Give one in appreciation for a hostess's hospitality.

Illustrate the covers with pressed flowers, collages or pictures from magazines. For titles, try calligraphy (see page 56) or use rubber stamps or your own handwriting.

INSTRUCTIONS

You need

- Large thick cardboard sheet
- Medium-weight paper for pages
- Metal ruler and triangle
- Illustration board or thick cardboard
- Artist's knife
- Rug or tapestry needle
- Dental floss or bookbinders' waxed linen thread
- Decorative paper or lightweight fabric
- Artist's paintbrush
- Decorative endpapers
- White glue
- Colored ribbon (optional)
- Burnisher or dull knife
- Flat, smooth work surface

To make

Protect work surface with large thick cardboard sheet. Refer to Fig. 1.

Cutting pages (folios) and cover boards

1. Measure paper for pages the length and twice the width you desire for your book. Be sure to measure pages accurately (Fig. 2). Mark ends of cutting lines by pricking paper with knife point at corners. Place metal ruler in line with knife pricks and draw knife along edge of ruler to cut straight edges. Each sheet you cut will be folded into 1 folio (4 pages); cut as many folios as desired for a small book.

2. Using same method, cut the 2 cover boards from illustration board. Make each ¼" longer than the folios and half as wide. Fold each folio in half and crease the fold with burnisher (Fig. 3). Place the folios 1 inside the other (Fig. 4).

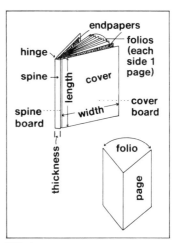

FIG. 1

FIG. 2

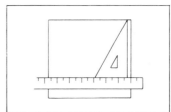

FIG. 3

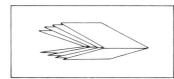

FIG. 4

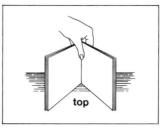

FIG. 5

Sewing the folios

1. Thread rug or tapestry needle with length of dental floss 2" to 3" longer than twice the length of book. Hold the lower edge of the folios in left hand with thumb along inside of fold. Turn folios over to tap top edge on flat surface; this will even the folios. Keep grip on folios and keep folios in the partly closed position shown in Fig. 5. (Figs. 6 and 7 show correct hand positions.) Begin sewing from the inside (Fig. 8).

2. Insert needle through fold from inside at center. Draw floss through, leaving about 2" of floss inside. Tap and align folios.

3. Insert needle through fold from outside at about ½" to 1" below upper edge of folios. Draw floss through to inside until it is flat against outside of fold.

4. Now insert needle through fold from inside at about ½" to 1" above lower edge of folios. Draw floss through until it is taut along inside of fold.

5. Insert needle from outside into center hole. Draw floss through until it is taut along outside of fold. Remove needle and tie a square knot with 2 ends of floss (Fig. 9). Trim floss ends to ½".

FIG. 6. Position of left hand for sewing folios

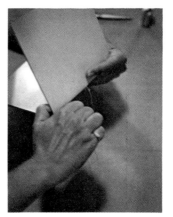

FIG. 7. Right hand position inserting needle from back to inside

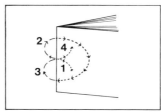

FIG. 8

Cutting spine board

With illustration board and same method as Cutting Pages, cut spine board same length as cover boards and ¼" wider than the thickness the finished book will be. To determine that thickness, place the stitched folios between the 2 cover boards and measure (Fig. 10).

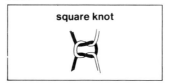

FIG. 9

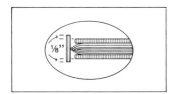

FIG. 10

Gluing spine and cover boards to cover material

1. Paper or fabric cover material must be ½" larger all around than spine and cover boards laid out as shown in Fig. 11. Place cover material face down on flat work surface. Place boards on cover material and mark positions on corners as shown in Fig. 11.

2. If desired, thin glue slightly with water. With artist's brush apply glue to spine and cover boards and place in position on cover material. Turn over and rub entire glued surface from outside with burnisher. Take special care to rub edges. Top with piece of scrap paper and press flat under weight of several heavy books until glue is dry. Trim corners of cover material as shown in Fig. 11.

3. Spread glue on cover boards at corner areas. Fold cover material over at corners as shown in Fig. 12. Spread glue evenly along lower edge of spine and cover boards (including lower edge of cover material between spine and cover boards).

4. Fold cover material up over glued edge and rub with burnisher to insure good contact (Fig. 13). Repeat on all edges. If ribbon page marker is desired, glue it to inside of spine. Press flat under weight as in step 1 until glue is dry. Make hinge between spine and cover board by creasing with burnisher.

Cutting and gluing endpapers

Endpapers are used to cover folded-over cover and spine material on inside of covers and to join folios to cover. Cut 2 endpapers from decorative paper the same length as the folios and 1" to 2" wider than the flat folios. Spread glue evenly on 1 cover board. Place 1 side of endpaper into position on inside of cover board so that an equal amount of cover material shows on 3 edges. Fold endpaper along inside edge of cover board. Repeat with second endpaper. (See Fig. 14.)

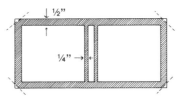

FIG. 11

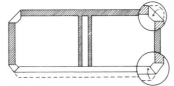

FIG. 12

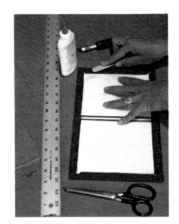

FIG. 13. Burnishing cover materials to cover boards

FIG. 14

Gluing book to endpapers

Spread thin film of glue along a ½"-wide strip on inside of each glued endpaper's folded edge (Fig. 15). Then spread thin film of glue along ½"-wide strip on front and back of outside folio at fold (Fig. 16). Hold folios in partly closed position and insert between endpapers so glue meets glue (Fig. 17). Sewn edge of book should touch spine board. Push glued surfaces together with burnisher.

Pressing book

Leaving spine free, as in Fig. 18, press book under weight for several hours, or even days, as determined by size and thickness of book.

Trimming endpapers

With metal ruler and artist's knife, trim away the 2 free endpapers (Fig. 19).

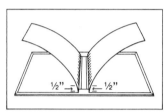

FIG. 15

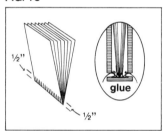

FIG. 16

FIG. 17. Inserting stitched folios between endpapers

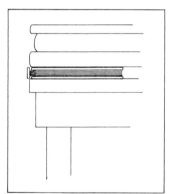

FIG. 18

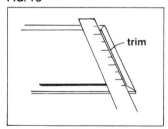

FIG. 19

Baskets

The art of basketry was originally a necessary industry among North American Indians and other primitive peoples. The talents and techniques of basket construction became family tradition and were handed down from generation to generation. Today, as baskets have become accessories rather than necessary containers, color and shape are open to a relaxed interpretation. Baskets lend their own special feeling of nature to any room in your house where the accent is on casual family living.

The splint method is one of the basic ways to make baskets. Early American colonists used flat strips of wood from local ash, hickory, oak and maple trees to weave these baskets, which were so important to their rugged way of life. Follow the step-by-step photographs as you go to see exactly how the basket is constructed. Later, add natural color and texture to your baskets by weaving in cattails, straw and/or raffia directly over the splints. Substitute branches of wild grape bark for splints, weaving in the same manner.

After you have become familiar with the splint basket technique, make a more advanced round basket of willow or reed. Many of the same principles are used to make both types. Though the base will be square the inherent quality of willow and reed will result in a round basket. For best results, use thin green branches from weeping willow trees as we did, or substitute round reed for willow.

BASKETRY TERMS

Base   The woven mat which forms the bottom of a splint basket.

Bone Awl   To make one, pound a large cooked, cleaned meat bone with a hammer so it splinters. Select one of the large splinters and file it smooth with a metal file.

Lashing   Narrow strip of splint which binds the rim to the woven part of the basket.

Rim   Several splints which are lashed together at top of basket.

Splints   Flat lengths of reed or ash which usually measure 5' x 6' long and ⅝" wide.

Spokes   Splints which form the framework or warp of the basket.

Weavers   Splints which are woven over and under the spokes.

SPLINT BASKET INSTRUCTIONS

You need

- Large tub or sink
- 1 lb. white ash or flat reed splints, each 5'-6' long x ⅝" wide (about 15)
- Card table or any work table suitable for wetting
- Sponge
- Needle-nosed wire clippers or kitchen shears
- Bone awl or strong knitting needle
- Ruler

To make

Keep splints damp while working with them. If you find you have made a mistake, take out all weaving back to mistake and continue from there. Be aware of the pressure you are exerting on spokes while weaving; pressure will affect the shape of the basket. On ash splints the smooth shiny side (step 2) is easily visible. To test for smooth side on flat reed, bend a wet piece of reed back and forth until splinters begin to pop up. The side that does not splinter is the smooth side. Step numbers in instructions correspond to Figure numbers.

1. Fill tub with warm, not hot water. Coil 7 splints loosely and soak in water for 2-5 minutes until pliable. Do not leave spokes in water longer than necessary; prolonged soaking makes them brittle. You may wish to soak fewer splints at a time if you are working slowly. With wet sponge, keep splints damp while weaving. Soak additional splints as needed.

2. Cut each of the 7 splints into 28" pieces (15 in all). Wet the top of the work table and place 3 splints, smooth shiny side up, hori-

FIG. 1

FIG. 2

FIG. 3

FIG. 4

FIG. 5

FIG. 6

FIG. 7

FIG. 8

FIG. 9

FIG. 10

FIG. 11

FIG. 12

FIG. 13

FIG. 14

FIG. 15

FIG. 16

zontally side by side on table with ¼" to ½" between spokes.

3. Weave 3 splints over 1, under 1 vertically through the 3 horizontal splints, keeping weaving centered as you work (Fig. 3A). Weave by sliding vertical splints in from ends of horizontal splints. Push splints as close together as you can but do not allow edges to meet. There should be ¼" squares (approximately) between woven splints.

4. Weave the remaining splints into the base, adding several horizontally and then several vertically so the base is a 6-splint x 8-splint rectangle. Always work from the center outward; use bone awl or knitting needle to push splints into position. When the base is complete, check to make sure weave is centered, adjusting splints until splint lengths are equal on opposite sides.

5. Turn base over so smooth shiny side is down. Place edge of ruler along 1 edge of base and gently bend all of the splints upward; repeat on all sides. This scores them and makes initial weaving easier.

6. Making first 3 weavers. Cut a well-soaked splint lengthwise into thirds.

7. Weave 1 weaver, rough side up, diagonally into the base to anchor it. Bend the weaver at a corner so shiny side is facing outward. Weave as in Fig. 3A through the spokes all around base once. Keep tension on weaver so weave isn't loose. While weaving, pull each 2 corner spokes into a vertical position. Maintain tension on weavers so these corner spokes will remain in position and guide basket sides vertically as you work.

8. After weaving around once, you will come to the spoke you wove over first. Stop and cut this initial spoke lengthwise down to base to form 2 spokes. This will give you the odd number of spokes you need to finish a weave. Weave through these 2 spokes and continue around a 2nd time; pattern will look like Fig. 3A.

9. Adding a 2nd weaver. Overlap the end of the old and new weavers for 2-3 spokes. The end of the new weaver is over the old weaver and hidden under a spoke. Weave around with 2nd and successive weavers, pushing weavers down to base. The pushing process should help keep the 1st weaver in place; if regularly applied, a neat weave will result.

10. Adding a half-width weaver. Cut a soaked splint lengthwise in half. Use as a weaver as in step 9, tapering its end for 4"-5" for smooth transition. (Fig. 10 shows twill weave; see Fig. 10A for diagram.)

11. Varying weaver sizes adds interest and design. Add a ⅝" weaver as in steps 9 and 10, using twill weave (Fig. 10A).

12. Continue weaving to desired height, leaving at least 2" free on spoke ends. Do the last 3 rounds with weavers cut in thirds (step 6) and ¼" spaces between spokes. If more than 2" is left, trim spokes to 2" so spokes can be woven back down to anchor top weaver.

13. Beginning rim. Select spokes on the inside of the basket under the top weaver (alternate spokes) and clip off each one at edge of top weaver with wire clippers or shears. Clip remaining spokes diagonally; score and bend them to inside of basket. Tuck each under 2-3 weavers on inside.

14. Wrap a soaked uncut splint around top edge of basket so ends overlap slightly. Cut 2 splints to fit edge. Lay 1 on inside and 1 on outside of basket edge. Cut a splint lengthwise into thirds; use 1 third as a weaver for lashing. With shiny side down, push weaver end down through space between 2nd and 3rd weavers until 1" of weaver is on inside of basket. Fold the 1" piece diagonally to the right and bring the long end of weaver up and over basket edge; poke end through from the inside out between the next 2 spokes on the right. Pull until tight, securing the tail of the weaver. Shiny side of weaver must be on outside.

15. Continue lashing all around basket. Tuck ends of rim splints under ends already lashed.

16. Lash to last available space between spokes. Carry lashing over the top and tuck down through several weavers on inside of basket. Clip off excess.

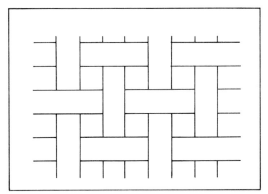

FIG. 3A

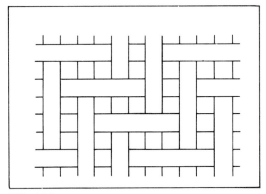

FIG. 10A

ROUND BASKET INSTRUCTIONS

You need

- Thin green branches from weeping willow trees, or 1 lb. each #4 and #1 round reed
- Pliers
- Bone awl or strong knitting needle

You need for reed only

- Large tub or sink
- Card table or any work table suitable for wetting
- Sponge

To make

If you are using reed, soak reed as in step 1 of Splint Basket Instructions.

1. With 8 lengths of willow or reed, weave a square 4-spoke x 4-spoke base as in steps 3 and 4 of Splint Basket Instructions. Jam 1 extra spoke into base to get the odd number of spokes needed for weaving. Pinch spokes at edge of base with pliers to flatten so they will bend easily.

2. With 2 willow or reed weavers together, weave as in Fig. 3A.

3. Reinforcing strength and keeping basket dense. Double the number of spokes by jamming extra spokes in after 1"-3" have been woven and thereafter as basket proceeds.

4. Controlling the basket's girth. Vary the tension exerted on spokes; put pressure on spokes from outside when you want basket to narrow; put pressure on spokes from inside when you want basket to widen.

5. Oblong openings. To leave oblong openings, do not weave all the way around; stop and start weaving in the opposite direction. Weave back and forth between openings until they are desired size, then begin to weave all around basket again.

6. Finishing. Weave last weavers down into basket and trim. Allow spokes to remain natural length at top of basket or trim to desired length.

Wedding Dress

Reach into the past and retrieve an old craft that revives traditional simplicity on your wedding day. Make your own dress, make your own day. Because you want it that way.

The special beauty of your dress is in the crewel embroidery. It's an art that has been practiced at least since the days of William the Conqueror, when the treasured Bayeux Tapestry was created. In the United States, the 18th century saw girls as young as six laboring over the tiny stitches of samplers, so when they reached marriage age they would be skilled enough to embroider their own bridal gowns. And that's just what they usually did.

The crewel on this gown captures the natural charm and serenity of Queen Anne's lace, lunaria, wheat shafts and mushrooms. Do them in white, beige and ecru, with accents in rust and rosy beige. Stitch in wool—wool is what distinguishes crewel from embroidery. Then use pearl cotton to add sheen.

Start with a simple dress in white country cotton or linen that you purchase or make with a pattern. Choose a dress whose lines are pure, a perfect foil for the crewel on the sleeves and hemline. The same dress in paisley fabric makes lovely bridesmaids' dresses.

INSTRUCTIONS

You need

- Wedding Dress Patterns (pages 194-195)
- Long A-line cotton or linen dress with broad sleeves
- Enlarging Patterns materials (see page 206)
- Transferring Patterns materials (see page 206)
- 1 ball each #5 pearl embroidery cotton in white and ecru
- 3-strand wool Persian yarn in the following colors:
    white
    very pale yellow
    beige
    light brown
    rosy beige
    rust
- Large-eye embroidery needle

To make

1. With Enlarging Patterns Materials, bring Wedding Dress Pattern 1 up to full size. With Transferring Patterns Materials, transfer design to front of dress skirt near hem.

2. With Enlarging Patterns Materials, bring Wedding Dress Pattern 2 up to full size. With Transferring Patterns Materials, transfer design to sleeve as shown in photograph; repeat for other sleeve.

3. With pearl cotton and all 3 strands of Persian yarn, work designs in stitches and colors designated with Patterns.

Wedding Cake

What's more important on a wedding table than the cake? Share with your guests this wedding cake that reflects the heritage of America and symbolizes the love you share with each other.

Standing in three tiers of four layers each, our countrified cake displays thistles, sunflowers and mushrooms—all meringue—and sliced-almond lunaria. Inside, there's a surprise! Cover six each date-nut and lemon pound cake layers with cranberry, apricot or plum filling, sprinkle with fruit liqueur, then stack them alternately. Ice the cake in coffee buttercream, a colorful partner to the chocolate leaves and stems of the decoration.

To make the layers, use cake mixes. Bake them up to three weeks before the wedding; then freeze them until decorating day. Make the meringue decorations a week before, and assemble, ice and decorate the cake the day before.

Cake decoration is easy when you know a few simple tips. Do not thaw the cake before decorating. Put the cake on a turntable, if you have one, and use a spatula (the raised-handle kind is best) to smooth the icing before you begin adding the trim.

When you're decorating, let the icing do the work; move your hand as little as possible. Stop squeezing the decorating bag just before the decoration you are making is fully formed. Lift up and away or down and away from the decoration as you stop squeezing, depending on which way the decoration will face. When making flower stems or other stringwork, keep the tube well away from and above the part of the cake on which you are working. The string will fall into position.

CAKES INSTRUCTIONS

Bake cakes at least 3 days before wedding; cakes can be frozen no longer than 1 month. Grease and flour two 12" round layer pans, two 10" round layer pans and two 8" round layer pans.

Date Bar Mix Cakes

You need
- Six 14-oz. packages date bar mix
- 3 cups hot water
- 12 eggs
- 6 teaspoons baking powder
- 3 cups chopped walnuts (about 16 oz.)

To make

Heat oven to 350°

1st cake

Mix date filling from 3 packages date bar mix and 1½ cups hot water. Stir in crumbly mix from 3 packages, 6 eggs, 3 teaspoons baking powder and 1½ cups chopped walnuts. Spread in one 12" pan. Bake 15 minutes. Decrease oven temperature to 325° and bake until top springs back when touched lightly with finger, about 45 minutes. Cool cake in pan or on large wire rack. Increase oven temperature to 350°.

2nd cake

Mix date filling from 2 packages date bar mix and 1 cup hot water. Stir in crumbly mix from 2 packages, 4 eggs, 2 teaspoons baking powder and 1 cup chopped walnuts. Spread in one 10" pan. Bake 15 minutes. Decrease oven temperature to 325° and bake until top springs back when touched lightly with finger, 35 to 40 minutes. Cool cake in pan or on large wire rack. Increase oven temperature to 350°.

3rd cake

Mix date filling from 1 package date bar mix and ½ cup hot water. Stir in crumbly mix from

1 package, 2 eggs, 1 teaspoon baking powder and ½ cup chopped walnuts. Spread in one 8" pan. Bake 15 minutes. Decrease oven temperature to 325° and bake until top springs back when touched lightly with finger, 30 to 35 minutes. Cool cake in pan or on wire rack.

Cut all thoroughly cooled cake layers horizontally in half. Wrap in plastic freezer wrap, label and freeze.

Pound Cake Mix Cakes

You need
- Four 16-oz. packages golden pound-cake mix
- 2⅔ cups water
- 8 eggs
- 4 teaspoons grated lemon peel

To make

Heat oven to 325°.

1st cake

Blend 2 pound-cake mixes, 1⅓ cups water, 4 eggs and 2 teaspoons lemon peel in large bowl on low speed, scraping bowl constantly, until moistened. Beat 3 minutes on medium speed scraping bowl occasionally. Spread in one 12" pan. Bake until wooden pick inserted in center comes out clean, about 1 hour 15 minutes. Cool cake in pan or on large wire rack.

2nd and 3rd cakes

Prepare as in 1st cake except measure 4⅔ cups batter into one 10" pan and 2⅓ cups batter into one 8" pan. Bake until wooden pick inserted in center comes out clean, 45 to 55 minutes. Cool cakes in pans or on large wire racks.

GOOD LUCK MERINGUES
INSTRUCTIONS

You need

- 2 baking sheets
- Brown paper
- 3 egg whites
- ¼ teaspoon cream of tartar
- ¾ cup sugar
- Medium round decorating tube
- Plastic decorating bag or parchment cone
- Spatula
- Cocoa
- Sharp pointed knife (optional)
- Small soft-bristle brush
- Shredded coconut
- Small round decorating tube
- 1 recipe Chocolate Decorating Icing (see below)

To make

Heat oven to 200°. Prepare at least 4 days before wedding; can be stored in tightly covered container no longer than 1 week. Makes about 100 mushrooms, 33 thistle crowns and 3 sunflower centers.

1. Cover 2 baking sheets with brown paper. With pencil, mark 1" rows on paper as guide for measuring mushrooms, thistles and sunflower centers.

2. Beat egg whites and cream of tartar until foamy. Beat in sugar, 1 tablespoon at a time; continue beating until stiff and glossy (Fig. 1). Do not underbeat.

3. Fit bag or cone with medium round decorating tube. With spatula, fill bag half-full with meringue; fold top of bag to keep meringue inside.
Mushroom caps. Hold tube upright and pipe one hundred ¾" rounds of meringue (Fig. 2); vary size for interest, if desired. Sprinkle generously with cocoa. Bake 35 minutes. Remove from oven; immediately turn caps upside down and with tube tip, make indentation in bottom of each cap (Fig. 3). If caps become too brittle to press, with sharp-pointed knife carefully carve out the bottoms.

FIG. 1

FIG. 2

FIG. 3

Brush off excess cocoa with soft-bristle brush; cool.

Mushroom stems and thistle crowns. On 2nd baking sheet, pipe one hundred ¾" upright cones. When piping, pull tube away so stems have peaks; these pointed ends fit the mushroom caps. For thistle crowns, hold bag at 45° angle and pipe thirty-three ¾" strips with a point at 1 end of each. Carefully press shredded coconut onto each crown. (See Fig. 4.)

Sunflower centers. Hold bag upright and pipe three ¾" rounds. If meringue is left over, make extra mushrooms. Bake 35 minutes. Remove from oven; cool.

4. Assembling. Fit decorating bag or cone with small round decorating tube. With spatula, fill bag half full with Chocolate Decorating Icing; fold bag to keep icing inside. Pipe a dot of icing into indentation of each mushroom cap; insert stem (Fig. 5). Set upside-down to dry. Store finished meringues in tightly covered container.

FIG. 4

FIG. 5

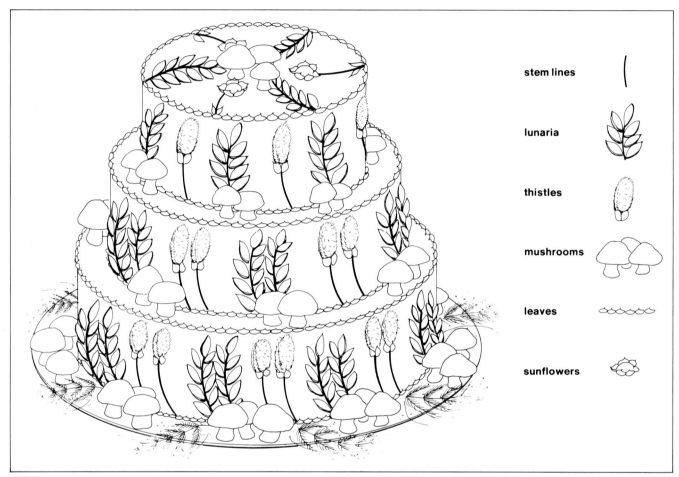

stem lines

lunaria

thistles

mushrooms

leaves

sunflowers

FIG. 6

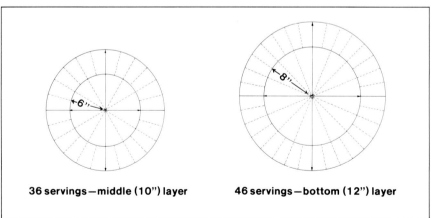

36 servings—middle (10") layer

46 servings—bottom (12") layer

cut along inner circle first, then into quarters

cut outer ring into slices, then inner ring into wedges

FIG. 7

ICINGS AND FILLINGS INSTRUCTIONS

Coffee Buttercream Icing

You need
- 4 cups butter, softened
- 8 lbs. confectioner's sugar
- 1½ cups hot strong coffee
- ¼ cup vanilla

To make

Make this recipe the day before wedding.

Mix butter and sugar. Stir in coffee and vanilla; beat until smooth and spreading consistency, stirring in additional coffee, 1 tablespoon at a time, if necessary. Use immediately.

Chocolate Decorating Icing

You need
- 1 cup shortening
- 3 tablespoons butter or margarine, softened
- 3 cups confectioner's sugar
- Dash salt
- 1½ teaspoons vanilla
- ¾ cup cocoa
- About 6 teaspoons hot water

To make

Beat shortening, butter, 1½ cups confectioner's sugar, salt and vanilla on low speed in mixing bowl until smooth. Gradually add remaining confectioner's sugar and cocoa. Stir in water, 1 teaspoon at a time, until icing is of spreading consistency.

Fillings

You need
- One 16-oz. can jellied cranberry sauce
- Two 30-oz. cans pitted apricots
- Two 16-oz. jars purple plums

To make

Cranberry filling

Stir the cranberry sauce to break it up.

Apricot filling

Drain apricots thoroughly; mash or sieve.

Plum filling

Drain and pit plums. Cut up very finely with scissors; drain well.

CAKE ASSEMBLY INSTRUCTIONS

You need
- All cakes, frozen
- ½ recipe Coffee Buttercream Icing
- All fillings
- About ¼ cup orange, peach or cherry liqueur

To make

Do not thaw cakes to assemble.

1. Place 1 split 12" date cake on large plate or platter; with spatula, ice top with thin layer of icing and spread with ½ cup Cranberry Filling. Sprinkle with liqueur. Top with 1 split 12" pound cake; ice top and spread with 1 cup Apricot Filling. Sprinkle with liqueur. Top with remaining 12" date cake; ice top and spread with 1 cup Plum Filling. Sprinkle with liqueur. Top with remaining 12" pound cake; sprinkle top with liqueur and ice.

2. Center 1 split 10" date cake on top; ice top and spread with ½ cup Cranberry Filling. Sprinkle with liqueur. Top with 1 split 10" pound cake; ice top and spread with ¾ cup Apricot Filling. Sprinkle with liqueur. Top with remaining 10" date cake; ice top and spread with ¾ cup Plum Filling. Sprinkle with liqueur. Top with remaining 10" pound cake; sprinkle top with liqueur and ice.

3. Place 1 split 8" date cake on 8" cardboard circle. Center cardboard atop cake. Ice top of 8" date cake and spread with ¼ cup Cranberry Filling. Sprinkle with liqueur. Top with 1 split 8" pound cake; ice top and spread with ¼ cup Apricot Filling. Sprinkle with liqueur. Top with remaining 8" date cake; ice top and spread with ¼ cup Plum Filling; sprinkle with liqueur. Top with remaining 8" pound cake; sprinkle with liqueur. Ice top and sides of entire cake with thin layer of remaining icing. Store uncovered no longer than 24 hours.

CAKE DECORATING INSTRUCTIONS

You need

- ½ recipe Coffee Buttercream Icing
- Decorating tubes as follows:
    small star tip
    small round tip
    medium leaf tip
- 2 plastic decorating bags or parchment cones
- 1 recipe Chocolate Decorating Icing
- Spatula
- Good Luck Meringues (see above)
- Waxed paper
- Sliced almonds

To decorate

1. Reserve ½ cup Coffee Buttercream Icing. With remaining icing, ice entire cake smoothly.

2. Fit 1 decorating bag or cone with small star tube; fit another bag or cone with small round tube. With spatula, fill bags or cones half full with Chocolate Decorating Icing. Fold top of bag to keep icing inside.

3. Decorate cake as in Fig. 6, beginning with top of cake and working down.

Stem lines. Use small round tube. Hold bag or cone at 45° angle; lift away from cake before line is completed.

Sunflowers. Practice on waxed paper before working directly on cake. Place meringue sunflower centers at ends of alternate stem lines atop cake. With leaf tube and icing, make petals around each center and leaves on the stems.

Lunaria. Push sliced almonds into icing on either side of remaining stem lines.

Mushrooms. If necessary, with small round tube and Coffee Buttercream Icing, pipe a dot on mushroom bases to help them adhere to cake.

Leaves. Practice on waxed paper before working directly on cake. With leaf tube, hold bag or cone straight up and pipe leaf to desired length; lift tube away. Begin next leaf at point of previous leaf.

Thistles. With star tube and Chocolate Decorating Icing pipe a small star on rounded end of each meringue thistle. Press thistles star end down into cake. If necessary, with small round tube and Coffee Buttercream Icing, pipe a dot of icing on the back of each thistle to help it adhere to cake.

4. Secure 10 groups of 3 medium mushrooms on the plate around cake bottom. Place remaining mushrooms in a basket beside cake (make a 2nd recipe if desired).

CAKE SERVING INSTRUCTIONS

You need

- Completed cake
- Long, sharp knife

To serve

Lift the top layer off and reserve for bride. With long, sharp knife cut cake as in Fig. 7. Remove mushrooms as cake is cut and serve 1 to each guest.

Embroidered Shirt

Decorate a casual denim shirt or a fine dressy blouse with embroidered flourishes of hearts and flowers. It's an ideal way to top anything from pants to a long skirt. Use all the motifs, as shown here, or choose one or just a few to add an extra touch of color to shirts, linens, jackets, jeans or any piece.

INSTRUCTIONS

You need

- Embroidered Shirt Patterns (pages 196-197)
- Enlarging Patterns materials (see page 206)
- Transferring Patterns materials (see page 206)
- 6-strand embroidery cotton in the following colors:

pink	lavender
blue	gold
light green	red
dark green	yellow
orange	white

- Embroidery needle(s)
- Embroidery hoops
- Shirt in solid color

To make

With Enlarging Patterns Materials, bring desired patterns in Embroidered Shirt Patterns 1-4 up or down to a size that will fit shirt. Size of shirt determines size of grid; if shirt pocket measures 3" across, reduce pocket pattern. With Transferring Patterns Materials, transfer full-size pattern(s) to shirt. Embroider shirt collar, cuffs, tabs and pockets according to stitches and colors given with Patterns. ○

Silkscreen Printing

The silkscreen process is one of the most versatile printing processes known. Materials for it are inexpensive, it is an easy technique to learn and it can be used to print on many different kinds of materials. Silkscreen printing is perhaps one of the easiest ways to generate multiple images in limited quantities. Materials are available at many art- and framing-supply stores.

Begin by taping over wooden frames on the purchased silkscreens, then shellac the taped area to make it water-resistant. A special type of film called profilm is used in silkscreen printing. For each color you will be printing, cut away the area on the film that will hold that color and adhere the film to its screen. Prepare a padded surface for stretching fabric during printing (use a flat surface for paper and wood printing), then plan exactly where on the fabric you will place the design. Make trial prints on paper until one is perfect, then print directly on fabric. When you have finished printing, clean your screens and save them for future projects.

Commercially, the silkscreen process is used for such diverse items as billboards, decals, ceramics, T-shirts, bumper stickers, pennants, road signs and many others. Many artists use it for printmaking, painting and sculpture. Use our bright and cheery apple design to print on fabric, as we have done, on paper to make friendly notes, or on wood that you can cut and sand to make a child's puzzle. Translate the design into other crafts, too, like quilting, stitchery or needlepoint. You can also use the apple outline alone to silkscreen with a solid color instead of stripes. And of course, once you know the technique you can print any design you desire with the silkscreen process.

SCREEN PREPARATION INSTRUCTIONS

You need

- Two 10" x 14" silkscreens
- 1½"-wide paper tape
- Shellac
- Paintbrush
- Silkscreen Pattern (page 197)
- Enlarging Patterns materials (see page 206)
- White drawing paper
- Pencil
- Profilm
- Masking tape
- Artist's knife
- Ruler
- Film adhering liquid
- Soft clean cloth
- Fine artist's paintbrush
- Stencil filler

To prepare

1. Tape over wooden frame on each screen as follows: On inside, seal corners with tape, then attach tape ½" over screen and up sides of frame. Continue taping over all of frame, also extending tape ½" over screen on outside. When dry, shellac. Extend shellacked surface ⅛" onto screen all around on both sides. Repeat process until tape is well shellacked and resistant to water—3-4 coats. Repeat with 2nd frame.

2. With Enlarging Patterns Materials and white drawing paper, bring Silkscreen Pattern up to full size. Tape drawing to flat surface. Cut piece of profilm slightly larger than screen and, with waxed side down, center film over drawing. Tape. With artist's knife and ruler, cut film only along lines around areas that will print red. Peel away cut film until all red stripes have been removed.

3. Adhering film to screen. Place film waxed side down; center screen on top of film. Apply a small amount of adhering liquid to clean cloth and, with circular motion, starting in center of screen, rub cloth firmly over screen a small section at a time. Do not apply too much liquid; film will dissolve. Work quickly; liquid reacts with film, causing it to stick to screen. Film will change color as it adheres. When liquid is dry and film is attached to screen, peel away waxed-paper backing.

4. With fine artist's paintbrush and stencil filler, touch up any areas where film did not adhere. Paint filler along edges of shellac.

5. Repeat steps 2-4 with 2nd screen for green stripes of apple.

WORK SURFACE PREPARATION INSTRUCTIONS

You need

- 4' x 8' porous wallboard
- Heavy-duty fabric tape
- Old blankets or padding material
- Large T-pins
- Old sheet

To prepare

Place porous wallboard on top of table, tape until secure. Center blanket or padding material on top of board. With T-pins, pin blanket ends to underside of wallboard, stretching evenly on all sides as you pin. Place sheet on top of padding and repeat stretching and pinning technique until finished surface is firm and taut.

FABRIC PRINTING INSTRUCTIONS

You need

- Shirt cardboard
- Pencil
- Tightly woven fabric
- Tape
- 2 T-pins or double-pointed jewelry pins
- Water-based textile inks in red and green
- Pad of newsprint paper
- Squeegee
- Old toothbrush
- Lacquer cleaning solvent

To print

1. (Plan position of apple designs carefully before applying ink.) With paper pattern from Screen Preparation Instructions and cardboard, make and cut out cardboard pattern. Place cardboard pattern on fabric and mark position with 2-3 pencil dots at edges of 2 or 3 red stripes; repeat wherever you want design to appear on fabric.

2. Aligning screen to fabric. Securely tape 2 T-pins (1 each) to outside of upper left and lower right corners of frame, with points extending below frame. Place clean red screen on fabric and align apple stripes on screen with those marked by pencil dots. When position is correct attach small piece of tape to fabric or padded surface under T-pin points. Press points into tape to mark holes to serve as guides while printing. Repeat process for all apples.

3. Trial prints. Open can of textile ink, stir with stick and put ink across top of screen a few inches above design. With newsprint, press screen against newsprint and, holding squeegee firmly, pull ink from top to bottom of screen. Never run squeegee over screen twice on any 1 print as this will cause ink to seep and blur print. You may need to make several trial prints before screen is flooded. Ink should be coming through screen only where film has been cut from design; if ink is coming through anywhere else, clean screen immediately with soap and water and cover holes with stencil filler; when dry, test screen again. After 1st perfect trial print is made, you are ready to begin.

4. Printing. Align pins with pin holes in tape on screen, squeegee red ink through screen, lift frame straight up and away from fabric, move on to next design and repeat. Move quickly and accurately. If there is a light print, clean screen immediately. Do not allow ink to dry on screen. If designs are placed close together, screen every other one to prevent frame from pressing against wet prints; let dry and print remaining designs. Let all dry thoroughly.

5. When printing is complete, clean screen and squeegee with soap, water and old toothbrush. With clean green screen, follow steps 2-4. Be sure to align screen perfectly on 2nd color; this is more important than inking.

6. To set inks, iron fabric following ink-manufacturer's instructions on ink can. When project is complete, clean screens with lacquer cleaning solvent to dissolve film so screens can be used again.

Candles

The flickering glow of cream-colored tapers cheered many a cold prairie night in pioneer days. Rendered animal fats left over from cooking were used to make candles then. Today, however, with paraffin from the grocery store, and beeswax and cotton braided wicking from candle-supply shops, you can easily make your own supply of these delicate candles.

Cut wicking into strips and tie the strips to short rods. Then boil water, insert a coffee can filled with ten parts paraffin to one part beeswax, and dip and re-dip the wicks until your candles reach the desired thickness. When completed candles are dry, untie the knots and your candles are ready for use.

The instructions below yield about 50 candles.

INSTRUCTIONS

You need

- 21 yds. wicking
- Seventeen 20"-long ¼" dowel rods
- 2 brooms or mops
- Newspapers
- Large pot
- 3-lb. coffee can, empty
- 6¼ lbs. paraffin
- 10 oz. beeswax
- Candy thermometer

To make

1. Cut wicking into strips as long as coffee can depth plus 6". Tie 3 wicks around each rod as in Fig. 1. Space wicks 2" apart (Fig. 2). Row of wicks should be no wider than coffee can.

2. Drying rack. Lay 2 brooms or mops across tops of 2 chairs as a drying rack and spread newspapers underneath to catch dripping wax.

3. Chandlering. Gently boil water in large pot. Put a few pieces of beeswax and paraffin into coffee can and lower can into water to form a makeshift double boiler. Do not allow water level to be so high that can floats. Can should rest on bottom of pot. As wax melts, gradually add remaining paraffin and beeswax. Gently

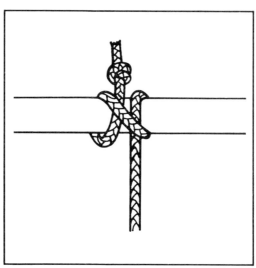

FIG. 1

stir with pencil or spare dowel to mix. Keep wax temperature 150°-160°—no higher—by checking with candy thermometer.

4. Hold a rod of wicks horizontally over the can. Lower wicks into can and then raise (Fig. 3). At this 1st dip, some wicks might float on surface, but as soon as they're wet with wax, they'll immerse. After 1st dipping, place rod on drying rack (Fig. 4) and straighten wicks by gently tugging at the bottom of each. Dip remaining wicks in same manner.

5. When all wicks have been dipped once, return to 1st set of wicks (which should be set) and dip again. Do not hold wicks in wax too long or 1st coat of wax will melt. Continue dipping and drying all wicks until candles reach desired thickness (Fig. 5). When wax in can gets low and coating the entire wick becomes difficult, add warm water to can; wax will float to the top for easier coating.

6. When finished candles are dry, untie knots and remove from rods. Trim wicks at both ends, leaving 1" wick at top of each candle.

FIG. 2

FIG. 3

FIG. 4

FIG. 5

Spin and Crochet Pillows

Spin wool yarn by hand; then crochet these shag pillows that combine a contemporary look and an old-fashioned spirit. It all starts with a wooden gadget called a Turkish drop spindle.

Purchase carded wool (the wool and the spindle are available at weaving-supply stores) and a piece of heavy spun yarn as a starter. When an arm's length of spun yarn accumulates, stop and wrap the yarn around the spindle arms. Repeat the process until spindle arms are two-thirds full. Then simply dismantle the spindle and you'll have a ball of yarn ready for dyeing and crocheting.

Dye the spun yarn a rich golden color with onion skin or any other color with household dye. Complete the pillows with a simple succession of double crochet rows and tie-on shag. Anything that's knitted or crocheted with yarn can be made with hand-spun yarn— knitted sweaters, crocheted afghans, woven rugs and much more.

SPINNING INSTRUCTIONS

You need

- 30" piece of heavy spun yarn
- Turkish drop spindle (available at weaving-supply shops)
- 8 oz. carded wool for each pillow

To make

As you gain experience, you can spin with spindle off the floor.

1. Tie the 30" piece of yarn onto one arm of the Turkish drop spindle. Wind yarn in and out of arms to secure; bring yarn up to top of shaft. Loop around shaft at notch with a backward loop. (See Fig. 1.)

2. Sit on the floor or in a low chair and place point of spindle on floor. Separate the fiber ends of the spun yarn, draw out a few fibers of a long, fluffy piece of carded wool (the rolag) and overlap the ends about 4". Hold together with thumb and forefinger of left hand.

3. With right hand placed about ⅓ the way down from top of spindle, turn the spindle in a clockwise direction, holding the join with left hand until spin accumulates. You will be able to see the spin accumulate in the yarn between the spindle and your left hand. (To get a kinky yarn, which is desirable for this project, give the spindle 1 or 2 extra spins until yarn begins to kink when released. By varying the amount of pull on fibers from time to time, you can spin a yarn of variegated thickness.) Stop spindle from spinning by lowering it to the floor. Do not allow spindle to turn in opposite direction. Move left hand up along rolag, bring right hand up near left hand, draw out fibers by gently pulling fibers between hands. Release fibers from right hand and start spindle again with right hand until desired amount of spin accumulates. Stop spin; then move right hand up again to draw out more fibers. Continue the spinning and drawing process; hands will move farther away from floor as more fibers are drawn out and spun.

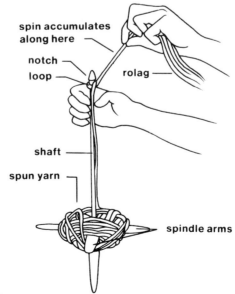

spin accumulates
along here

notch

loop

rolag

shaft

spun yarn

spindle arms

FIG. 1
SPINNING WITH A TURKISH SPINDLE

4. When you have spun about an arm's length, undo loop at top of shaft. Wind the spun yarn around the spindle arms in an under-over pattern, occasionally going under 2 arms for even distribution. Leave enough spun yarn unwound to loop around shaft at notch. Continue spinning until spindle arms are ⅔ full.

5. To remove yarn, dismantle spindle by pulling arms apart. Yarn will be in a ball ready to work.

CROCHET INSTRUCTIONS

You need

- 8 oz. spun yarn of variegated thickness for each pillow
- Size K crochet hook
- ½ yd. muslin
- 1-2 lb. polyester fiber stuffing

Gauge

5 sts = 2"
1 row = ⅞"

To make Gold-and-White Pillow

1. Dye 4 oz. yarn, following Dyeing Instructions below or using household dye.

2. Pillow Front. With undyed yarn and size K crochet hook, ch 31, making last ch long enough to be connecting ch between rows. Beg in 1st ch from hook, dc 1 in each ch across, ch 1 to turn. Repeat dc row and ch 1 until there are 14 rows. Fasten off. Block to a 12" square by pinning to ironing board and gently steaming. Do not press.

3. Repeat step 2 with undyed yarn for pillow back.

4. Cut remaining yarn into 6" lengths, reserving ½ ball gold yarn for assembling pillow. Tie gold and white yarn to Pillow Front in desired abstract pattern as follows: Fold a 6" length in half to form loop, insert crochet hook under dc st, pull loop under st, sl yarn ends through loop and pull tight. Tie 1 length of yarn to each dc st. Trim pile evenly.

5. With Pillow Front and Back wrong sides tog, sc edges closed along 3 sides with dyed yarn. Stitch muslin into a square to fit inside crochet casing (about 12" on a side), leaving 1 side open. Fill muslin with polyester stuffing and stitch closed. Slide muslin into crochet casing; sc casing closed.

To make White Pillow

Follow step 2 above; make 2. With white yarn, follow step 4 above, except cut yarn into 4" lengths and leave patches of pillow free of yarn ties. Follow step 5 above.

DYEING INSTRUCTIONS

You need

- 4 oz. spun wool
- ½ lb. onion skins
- 2 oz. alum (potassium aluminum sulfate)

To make

1. Wind yarn into 4 loose skeins. Tie each skein loosely with a contrasting yarn.

2. Soak onion skins overnight in an enamel pot with enough water to cover. Bring skins to a boil and simmer for 1 hour. Strain liquid by pouring through cheesecloth into large enamel pot; discard onion skins. Add 2 gallons water and 2 oz. alum to dye concentrate; stir to dissolve.

3. Soak yarn in clear water to saturate. Gently squeeze excess water from yarn, add yarn to dye bath and simmer for 1 hour, stirring occasionally. Remove yarn from dye, rinse in clear water and hang to dry. Wind yarn into balls.

Tile-Lined Tray and Stand

Today's version of the traditional butler's tray vibrates with color and appeals with sleek design, for you craft it of warm red oak and line it with painted tiles. Then it's ready for use as a portable bar or snack stand, a TV tray or a patio standby. The removable tray has built-in handles and the lightweight but sturdy stand serves without the tray as a handsome luggage rack.

Sand and rub the solid-wood stand to a warm, earthy luster; then link its legs with straps of webbing. The oak is easy to saw and piece, and the stand has the clean look afforded by dowel construction. Supplies are available at lumber-supply, hardware, tile-supply and art-supply stores. Be sure to purchase china paints that can be fired in the oven.

To create the convenient ceramic surface, begin with ordinary white bath tiles and paint them in our flower-and-butterfly graphic. The strokes of your brush become an integral part of the design. Use paints straight from the bottles or mix colors to create new shades. You can also follow our techniques and create your own design or, if you prefer, skip the painting step entirely and just use any purchased 4¼" square tiles to finish the table.

The finished height of the tray stand is 31". The finished tray measures 23¼" x 19" x 3".

TRAY AND STAND INSTRUCTIONS

You need

- Tray Pattern (page 198)
- One 7½" x ¾" x 36" red oak board and two 5½" x ¾" x 36" red oak boards
- Circular saw
- Plane or jointer
- Ruler
- Pencil
- Electric drill with ⅟₁₆", ¼", ¾" and 1" bits
- Coping saw or jigsaw
- 180 grit sandpaper
- Plastic resin wood glue
- Bar clamp
- One 3" x 24" x ¾" piece of pine
- One 24" x 24" piece ¼"-thick sliced red oak plywood (birch back)
- 1 pint linseed oil
- Soft cloth
- 1 pint white shellac
- Pencil compass
- Wood file or 80 grit sandpaper
- No. 0000 steel wool
- 1 teaspoon walnut stain
- Two each ¾" and 1" dowel rods, one 19⅜" long and one 20¾" long
- Two ¾" x ¼" round head screw with nuts
- Tape measure
- 5' length of 2"-wide non-stretch white cotton webbing
- 8 No. 6 x ¾" flat head screws with 8 countersunk washers
- Scrap of felt
- Scrap of ¾" dowel rod
- Paste wax
- 1 pint denatured alcohol

To make

With circular saw, rip (cut across lengthwise grain) oak boards for tray sides and ends and stand legs according to Tray Pattern. With plane or jointer, plane boards smooth along edges to 3" wide. With circular saw, cut tray ends to 17½" length and sides to 23¼" length. Plane legs smooth along edges to 2" wide. Set aside legs.

Tray

1. Handle holes. Mark and drill two 1" oval handle holes in each tray end, positioned as in Fig. 1. With coping saw, cut out wood between holes for handles. Sand sides and ends smooth, including oval handle holes.

2. Fit boards together to form rectangle as in Fig. 2. With plastic resin wood glue, glue together, making sure corner-to-corner dimensions are identical so tray will be square. With bar clamp, clamp sides; let glue dry.

3. Tray bottom supports. With circular saw, rip four ⅜"-square pine strips from ¾" pine. Cut strips to fit inside bottom of tray as in Fig. 2. Sand strips; glue in place along inside bottom edge of tray. Let dry.

4. Tray bottom. Measure interior of tray from top and with fine-tooth saw, cut ¼" plywood to fit as tray bottom. With glue mixed to a thick consistency, glue tray bottom to tray bottom supports. Let dry.

5. Sand tray. With soft cloth, rub 2 coats linseed oil over entire tray surface. Mix solution of 3 parts white shellac and 1 part linseed oil; with No. 0000 steel wool and solution, polish tray. Set tray aside.

Tray Stand

1. Cut each leg to 34" length. Cut bottom end of each leg off at a 59° angle. Round off top by marking with compass; cut along marks. File and sand top of legs smooth. Drill ¾" holes for dowels through legs 6" from bottom and 1" holes for dowels (rounds) through legs 1⅛" from top, positioned as in Fig. 1. Sand legs smooth. Apply 2 coats linseed oil; let dry. Apply shellac and linseed oil solution as in step 5 above.

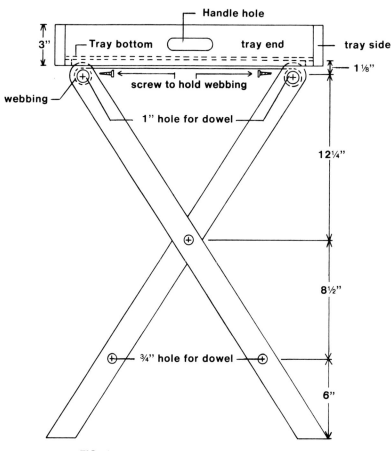

FIG. 1
TRAY/STAND SIDE VIEW

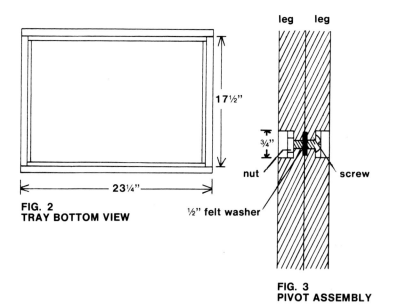

FIG. 2
TRAY BOTTOM VIEW

FIG. 3
PIVOT ASSEMBLY

2. Mix a solution of 1 teaspoon walnut stain and 4 teaspoons linseed oil. Dip ends of all 4 dowels into solution to depth of ½" and wipe off excess solution. Rub dowels with linseed oil.

3. Pivot point on legs. Drill a ¾" hole ⁷⁄₁₆" deep on 1 side of each of the 4 legs, positioned as in Fig. 1. Be sure to drill the holes so they will be on opposite sides when legs are crossed. Drill a ¼" hole through center of each ¾" hole as shown in Fig. 3.

4. Dry assembly. Dry assemble the stand as in Fig. 1, fastening with round head screws at pivot point as in Fig. 3. Lay bar clamp across top rounds to retain legs in open position. Adjust clamp so top of legs are spread to fit nicely into underside of tray.

5. Webbing. With tape measure, measure length of webbing needed. Webbing should reach between 1" rounds going over top of round, across tray, down around opposite round and back up toward top, as in Fig. 1. Allow ½" for folding under on each end. Cut 2 lengths of webbing to this measurement. Drill

two ¹⁄₁₆" holes 1" apart through each folded end of webbing and into round; fasten webbing to rounds with flat head screw and counter-sunk washers.

6. Disassemble legs. Cut two ½" round felt washers and place 1 between each pair of legs. Reassemble legs, using glue at all dowel joints. Let dry.

7. Measure space between ends of screw and edge of legs at pivot point. Cut dowel plugs (from ¾" dowel scrap) to exact length. Glue in place as in Fig. 3. Sand plugs smooth. Darken with walnut stain solution and apply linseed oil as in step 5 of Tray Instructions.

8. Polish entire surface of stand and tray with steel wool; apply coats of thin shellac. When dry, apply wax with steel wool and with soft cloth, buff. To assemble, simply place tray on stand.

TILE INSTRUCTIONS

You need

- Tile Pattern (page 199)
- 23¼" x 19" or larger sheet of tracing paper (pieced if necessary)
- Pencil
- Ruler
- Pink chalk
- Twenty-two 4¼"-square white glazed bath tiles
- Soft cloths or rags
- Brush cleaner
- Masking tape
- Oven-fireable china paints as follows:
    blue
    light blue
    red
    light red
    purple
    light purple
    green
    light green
    yellow
- Paint thinner for china paints
- Wooden ice cream sticks
- Muffin tin or other disposable paint pots
- Assorted flat paintbrushes, nos. 1-4
- 1 artist's pointed brush
- Cotton swabs (optional)
- Boilproof glaze and boilproof glaze thinner
- Boilproof-glaze thinner
- New 1½" paintbrush
- 1 small can wood sealer
- White glue
- Grouting compound
- Rubber spatula (optional)

To make

1. With tracing paper, ruler and pencil, draw grid of 4¼" squares. Draw Tile Pattern on grid. Rub chalk on back of tracing paper so it covers all design lines to make "carbon paper."

2. On a clean, flat surface in a well-ventilated area, arrange 20 tiles, edges touching, in a rectangle of 5 tiles horizontally x 4 tiles vertically. With cloth dipped in brush cleaner, clean tiles carefully to remove all traces of grease, dirt and fingerprints so paint will adhere.

3. Place drawing chalk-side down over tiles so tile lines on drawing match actual tile edges. Tape drawing securely to work surface, making sure tape does not touch tile surfaces. With pencil, draw over all design lines on tracing paper; a very light chalk line will transfer to tiles. Do not rub hand over design or tiles will be smudged. If desired, to minimize smudging and simplify transfer, transfer flower design to tiles first; remove tracing paper; cut out individual butterflies from tracing paper and transfer each to a single tile.

4. Painting tiles. Stir paints with ice cream stick. Pour small amount of paint (enough to cover area to be painted) into muffin tin or paint pot. Dip brush into paint thinner; then wipe on edge of bottle. Use 2 extra tiles to test colors and brushstrokes of all paintbrushes. Blend paint by working it with brush on any clean non-porous surface such as top edge of muffin tin. Stroke paint onto tile following chalk lines; paints will not be affected by chalk. (Paints dry rapidly as you work.) Clean brush after each color by dipping into brush cleaner and wiping with cloth. Apply paints in coats: 1 coat for light translucent hue and 2 or more coats for opaque colors. To remove part or all of a design, allow it to dry; then with cloth or cotton swab dipped in brush cleaner, wipe away. Rechalk lines that rub away while working. Paint entire design. Discard muffin tin or pots. Let tiles dry overnight.

5. Baking. Place painted tiles on racks in clean oven. Close door and set oven at 300°. Heat tiles 30 minutes; begin timing when oven is turned on. Turn oven off; open door and pull racks out. Let tiles cool on open oven racks for 2 hours. Wipe tiles with clean dry cloth to remove dust.

6. Glazing. Pour boilproof glaze into jar lid or other clean shallow container. With new brush, apply thin coat of glaze on each tile, stroking glaze in 1 direction only and covering entire surface. (Too much glaze might cause colors to bleed slightly.) Let glaze dry overnight. Repeat baking process in step 5.

7. Mounting. Apply wood sealer to tray surface; let dry. Apply white glue to tray surface and arrange tiles in tray, leaving equal spaces between. Let dry 12 hours. Fill in with grouting compound using rubber spatula or fingers to avoid scratching tiles. Wipe away excess grout following manufacturer's instructions. Let grout dry before using tray. ○

Filet Lace Curtains

Weave acrylic yarns through casement fabric to create a garden illusion in shades of white for your window. Apply the design to the entire curtain or only to a part of it; either way, light will shine through the openwork pattern to offer privacy with prettiness. For variety, use differing textures and weights of yarn. To finish, hand stitch a casing at the top and insert a curtain rod for hanging.

INSTRUCTIONS

You need

- Graph paper (geometric curtain only)
- White casement fabric to size of window plus 2" extra on each edge
- Tapestry needle
- Lightweight 2-ply white and off-white acrylic yarn and white bulky soft yarn
- Needle and cotton thread to match casement fabric
- Curtain rod

To make floral curtain

1. Determine position of design in Fig. 1 on casement fabric and number of times it will repeat.

2. Thread tapestry needle with yarn and weave design into fabric according to grid, counting 1 fabric square for each grid square in Fig. 1. With basic over-under-over weaving stitch, fill in casement squares.

3. Finishing curtain. Turn under 2" along side and bottom edges to wrong side of curtain, making sure to line up casement threads. With needle and cotton thread, hand stitch hem in place along casement thread with overcasting stitch or running stitch. Stitch threads within hem border together with running stitch to keep casement threads aligned. Hand stitch casing at top of curtain for curtain rod.

To make geometric curtain

On graph paper, plot desired geometric design to fit exact number of squares on fabric. (Working with a diagonal design is best.) Fill in squares and rectangles on graph paper to show where design will be woven. Follow procedure in steps 2 and 3 of Floral Curtain to complete curtain.

FIG. 1
REPEATING
FLORAL CURTAIN DESIGN

Tie-Dye

Bright colors in bold patterns are the hallmarks of tie-dyeing. The presence or absence of color is the basic principle of this versatile craft.

Begin this project by pleating the butterfly pattern areas, then tying them off with a rubber band and splashing with bright blues and turquoises. Then dip the tied fabric in a darker color—like our purple—to create a total design. When the fabric is dry, untie it to expose the unique and often surprising designs. Dye fabric before cutting and stitching.

Any fabric that will hold the dye is ideal for tie-dyeing. Dye raw fabric and use it with a commercial pattern to make a romantic kimono. It's also an easy and attractive way to perk up old T-shirts, canvas chairs and other single-colored fabric items. For a major decorating project, tie-dye fabric for curtains, draperies or bedspreads.

INSTRUCTIONS

You need

- Tie-Dye Pattern (page 199)
- 8½" x 11" piece of paper
- Felt-tip pen
- 45"-wide white acetate satin to yardage on pattern envelope, plus some extra
- Liquid dye in turquoise, royal blue and purple
- Rubber bands
- 3 plastic squeeze bottles, eyedroppers or spoons
- Large enamel pot
- Commercial pattern for garment

To make

Dye fabric yardage first; then cut and stitch garments. When dyeing heavier fabric, use larger design. Tie a few samples with extra fabric to determine the best size for the butterfly; 9" across is recommended for satin.

1. Bring Tie-Dye Pattern up to full size on piece of paper; cut out to use as pattern.

2. Wet fabric thoroughly in cool water and hang to drip almost dry, or put it through the spin cycle in a washing machine. Fabric should be damp so it will absorb dye easily and tie without slipping.

3. For each butterfly, fold fabric and place straight line of pattern on fold (Fig. 1A). Mark dotted outline with felt-tip pen (Fig. 1B). Gather both thicknesses of fabric along outline between thumb and forefinger into ½" pleats (Fig. 1C) and hold tightly in place with rubber band. Pleat both edges of butterfly tail simultaneously for an accurate outline (Figs. 1D and 1E); then fold together (Fig. 1F) and wind tightly with a rubber band so outline is covered (Figs. 1G and 1H) to make knot. Exaggerate butterfly shape slightly while pleating. Tie several butterflies into fabric by this method, varying placement of butterflies by folding fabric at different angles and spacing butterflies 12" or more apart.

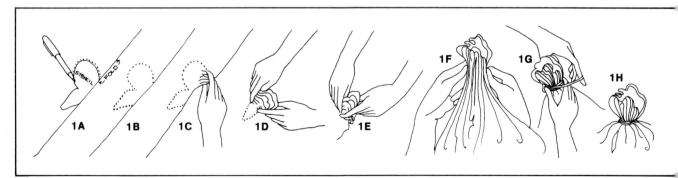

FIG. 1
TYING THE BUTTERFLY

4. With squeeze bottle, drip small amounts of undiluted turquoise and royal blue liquid dye on knotted fabric (Fig. 2A). Wind several rubber bands to the top of each knot and drop purple liquid dye around base of each knot (Fig. 2B).

5. After all butterflies are tied, make curved designs called <u>streamers</u> between them at random positions. With squeeze bottle, eyedropper or spoon, draw a curved line with turquoise dye for each streamer (Fig. 3A). Gather along line between thumb and forefinger into ½" pleats (Fig. 3B). Fold fabric (Fig. 3C) and fasten tightly with at least 2 rubber bands (Fig. 3D). Apply a generous amount of turquoise dye to knotted fabric (fabric will have runny look) (Fig. 3E).

6. Fill large enamel pot with water and heat to just below simmer. Dissolve remaining purple dye in water. Submerge tied fabric in dye solution and stir so fabric is thoroughly penetrated. Allow fabric to remain in dye for ½ hour at just below simmer, stirring constantly. Remove fabric and rinse in cold running water until water runs clear. Remove rubber bands and rinse again until water runs clear. Spin fabric in washing machine to remove excess water. Iron while still damp. Fabric is now ready for sewing garment.

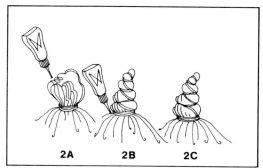

FIG. 2
ADDING DYE

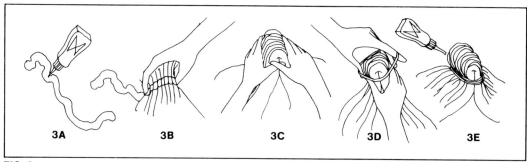

FIG. 3
TYING WITH STREAMERS

Quickpoint Bricks

Quickpoint is the same as needlepoint except you use a canvas that takes only five stitches to the inch. To fill this larger mesh, very heavy wools are used. The technique is almost always used for rugs, and is ideal for children's stitchery projects.

Use this fast and easy technique to cover bricks with quickpoint in our tulip or ribbon design. Complement your decor by using the bricks as doorstops; pairs of quickpoint bricks also make attractive and extra-special bookends for any library or bookshelf.

INSTRUCTIONS

You need for each brick

- Quickpoint Pattern (page 200)
- 1 piece 5 mesh quickpoint canvas 12" x 15"
- Masking tape
- 1 large-eyed blunt-tipped yarn needle
- Tapestry yarn as follows:
    For Tulip Brick:
    4 skeins yellow; ½ skein each orange, light orange, dark green, light green and pink
    For Ribbon Brick:
    1 skein each orange, bright green, chartreuse, purple, lavender, red and turquoise
- Brick
- Needle and heavy-duty thread
- 1 piece black felt, 8½" x 4"

To make

1. Bind edges of canvas with masking tape. Thread yarn needle with 4 strands of yarn or enough to cover mesh completely. Work Tulip or Ribbon design according to Quickpoint Pattern using continental stitch.

2. When quickpoint is complete, block canvas.

3. Place quickpoint over brick, folding at corners so quickpoint edges meet. With needle and heavy-duty thread, whipstitch edges together at corners. Turn brick over so blank side faces up. Place felt on blank side; whipstitch edge of felt to edge of quickpoint.

Hand Soap

Making your own soap is like making your own bread. The house is filled with a fresh "homemade" smell, the resulting product is natural and pure and there is great satisfaction in being able to create something so essential to life. You cannot buy the benefits you get from homemade soap: a rich, creamy lather free from harsh additives, a mildness that's wonderful for your skin and a clean soothing fragrance.

Until the 19th century, Americans saved huge quantities of fat from cooking and butchering, then mixed it with lye leached from wood ashes to make soap. The result was a soft, brown soap with a rancid odor. In 1806 William Colgate bought a vat that held 45,000 pounds of ingredients and began to make soap on a large scale. By the early 20th century there were many soap companies and soap bars were common items on store shelves.

The first step in soapmaking is rendering the fat. Obtain the beef fat from your butcher. Most will give it to you, but some might charge; never pay more than 15 cents per pound and ask for large, clean white pieces with as little meat attached as possible.

Divide the work into two days; render the fat on the first day and prepare the soap on the second. Plan to spend an entire morning or afternoon in the kitchen on the day you make the soap. The process usually takes about two hours, but might take longer. Use only stainless steel, enamel or heat-resistant glass for all utensils; lye can corrode tin, aluminum and other materials. All equipment can be used again for food preparation. Simply wash each utensil in hot, soapy water immediately after using it.

Once you've made basic white soap, you'll want to experiment with scents and colors. Choose essential oils for your scents such as oils of jasmine, lemon, lavender, pine balsam, almond or orange. Candle scents are too strong and cologne or toilet water might cause the soap mixture to separate because they contain alcohol. For color, candle dyes, powdered spices or flavorings and food coloring all work well. Like scent, however, color weakens as soap dries and ages. Candle dyes produce the truest colors; spices and

other foodstuffs quite often produce unexpected color results.

To personalize your soap you might want to use a variety of molds. Plastic molds for shaping candles and plaster of Paris, trays from cookie packages, household containers for bleach and detergent, spray-can lids and soap dishes are all marvelous shapes. Be certain, though, that the container you choose is at least as wide on the top as it is on the bottom. Glass or stainless steel molds need to be coated smoothly with vegetable oil or petroleum jelly before pouring soap in. Most metal molds will corrode unless you spray them with a plastic spray fixative, then coat with oil or jelly.

INSTRUCTIONS

You need

- 15 pounds clean beef fat
- Deep, 2- to 3-gallon pot
- 1 quart tap water
- 2 tablespoons salt
- Stainless steel spoon (preferably slotted)
- Large bowl
- Colander lined with 3 layers cheesecloth
- Newspapers
- Rubber gloves
- 5 cups cold soft water
- 2 heaping tablespoons borax
- One 13-oz. can lye
- 8-cup bowl or pot, with pouring lid
- Candy or deep-fat thermometer (preferably one that reads down to 75°)
- 2 pounds lard
- Plastic garbage bag
- Stapler
- 12" x 20" x 6" cardboard box or decorative mold
- 1-1½ oz. essential oil (optional)
- Powdered candle dye, spice or food coloring (optional)
- Glass measuring cup (optional)
- Towel or small rag
- Large knife
- Paring knife

To make

Use only stainless steel, enamel or heat-resistant glass for all utensils; lye can corrode tin, aluminum and other materials.

Rendering the fat

Trim off meat, then cut fat into stew-sized chunks. In large pot, mix 1 quart water and the salt and bring to a boil. Add chunks of fat and partially cover pot, lowering heat to a simmer. Simmer, stirring occasionally, for 4 hours. Strain the mixture into large bowl through cheesecloth-lined colander. Let cool to room temperature; cover and store in refrigerator. Clean pot thoroughly.

Making the soap

1. With newspaper, cover all work areas; lye is caustic and might mar floors and counters. Put on rubber gloves to protect hands.

2. Mixing lye. Pour 5 cups cold water and the borax into the 8-cup container. Add lye crystals (see Fig. 1); do not inhale fumes. The temperature of this mixture will reach about 160°; let cool to 85° (about 1 hour).

3. Mixing tallow and lard. While lye mixture is cooling, remove the rendered fat from refrigerator. It will be in 2 layers, a solid creamy layer of tallow on top and a jellied sediment on the bottom. Dislodge tallow from bowl; scrape off jellied sediment from below and discard. Put tallow into large pot and heat until it melts; pour off all but 10 cups. (Save the leftover tallow for another soapmaking; it will keep in the refrigerator for several weeks.) Melt lard at low heat; pour off all but 3½ cups. (Save leftover lard.) Add liquid lard to tallow, heat over a low flame and stir occasionally to blend (Fig. 2). Remove from heat and cool to 110°.

FIG. 1

FIG. 2

FIG. 3

FIG. 4

FIG. 5

FIG. 6

4. Preparing soap mold. Cut garbage bag into 1 layer and line cardboard box with it, stapling plastic along the top edges of the box. If desired, prepare other type of mold (see introduction).

5. Bring lye mixture to a temperature of 85° by placing container in a bowl of hot water to increase temperature or in a bowl of cold water to decrease temperature. Bring fat mixture to a temperature of 110° by cooling at room temperature or, if too cool, heating slowly until 110° is reached: never refrigerate or plunge the pot of fat into cold water to save time.

6. Combining lye and fat mixtures. (Have someone assist you at this point.) When both mixtures are at the correct temperatures, pour the lye very slowly and steadily (almost at a trickle) into the fat, gently stirring fat as you pour (Fig. 3). Little bubbles will rise to the top; this is saponification, the soap-making process. The mixture will soon smell soapy. Continue to stir after adding all of the lye until the mixture is the texture of fudge and a spoon pulled through it leaves a wake. Do not scrape residue from the sides.

7. Scenting. If desired, add 1 to 1½ oz. essential oil to soap mixture at this point (Fig. 4). Make quick circular motions with your spoon so that the oil is absorbed; be thorough as scent tends to form pockets.

8. Coloring. If desired, add coloring to soap mixture at this point after adding desired scent. Spoon out ½ cup soap mixture into glass measuring cup; add ½ teaspoon powdered candle dye, ½ teaspoon spice or other foodstuff or 1 teaspoon food coloring and blend thoroughly. Return tinted soap and coloring to large pot of soap by teaspoonfuls, stirring constantly to ensure even, uniform coloring (Fig. 5).

9. Molding. Gently pour soap mixture into mold (Fig. 6). Cover with towel or small rug; do not let the cloth touch the cooling mixture. Let cool for about 24 hours; do not peek under towel. (If soap cools too fast pockets of lye will form and batch will be unusable.)

10. Aging. When soap is firm but not brittle, with paring knife cut into bars. Remove from mold. Separate bars and let air dry. After at least 3 weeks, with paring knife scrape off any ash that has formed; soap can now be used or aged longer.

11. Finishing. With paring knife, smooth and square the sides of each bar. Make sure all planes are level and corresponding sides match. If desired, with paring knife carefully scrape bottom and top edges to 45° angles to bevel, then repeat process to bevel corners.

12. Carving. If desired, with sharp paring knife carve initials, geometric patterns or any desired design into soap.

Embroidered Sweater

This classic peasant-style cardigan has a strong Eastern European influence. Three techniques — knitting, crochet and embroidery — and the resulting variety in textures combine deftly to give the sweater high visual interest.

Knit it in warm wools and bright colors, crochet the edging and then embroider the floral design with needlepoint yarns. Give an old sweater new life by dressing it up with this floral design, too.

INSTRUCTIONS

Sizes

Instructions are for misses size 8 with changes for sizes 10, 12, 14, 16 and 18 in (   ).

Finished measurements

Garment width around underarms 35" (37", 39", 41", 43", 45)

Gauge

6 sts = 1"
8 rows = 1"

You need

- 9 (9, 9, 10, 10, 10) 1¾-oz. balls green (mc) and 1 ball red (cc) medium-weight 100%-wool sport yarn
- 10 yds. each 100% wool needlepoint-crewel yarns in light blue, rose, red, light green and gold
- No. 5 knitting needles (or size that will give proper gauge)
- Double-pointed (cable) needle (same size as knitting needles)
- Six ⅝" buttons
- No. 3 steel crochet hook
- Embroidered Sweater Patterns (page 201)
- Blunt yarn needle

To knit

Back

With mc and no. 5 needles, co 105 (111, 117, 123, 129, 135) sts.
Row 1 (right side): *P 15 (16, 17, 18, 19, 20), k 3* 5 times, ending p 15 (16, 17, 18, 19, 20). Rows 2, 4, 6 and 8: *K 15 (16, 17, 18, 19, 20), p 3* 5 times, ending k 15 (16, 17, 18, 19, 20). Row 3 and all wrong-side rows: *P 15 (16, 17, 18, 19, 20), sl 1 onto dp needle and hold in front of work, k 2, k 1 st from dp needle* 5 times, end p 15 (16, 17, 18, 19, 20). Repeat rows 1-8 for pat. Work until 16" from beg or desired length to underarm. Mark last row.
Shape Armholes. Keeping to pat, bind off 5 (6, 6, 7, 7, 8) sts at beg of next 2 rows. Dec 1 st each edge every other row 6 (6, 7, 7, 8, 8) times—83 (87, 91, 95, 99, 103) sts. Work even until armholes measure 7" (7¼", 7½", 7¾", 8", 8¼") above marked row.
Shape Shoulders. Keeping to pat, bind off at beg of each armhole edge 7 (7, 7, 8, 8, 8) sts 3 times, then 6 (7, 8, 6, 7, 8) sts once. Bind off rem 29 (31, 33, 35, 37, 39) sts.

Left Front

With mc and no. 5 needles, co 63 (66, 69, 72, 75, 78) sts. Row 1 (right side): *P 15 (16, 17, 18, 19, 20), k 3* 2 times, p 15 (16, 17, 18, 19, 20), put a marker on needle, *k 1, p 1* to end of row for front border. Row 2: *P 1, k 1* to marker, k 15 (16, 17, 18, 19, 20), *p 3, k 15 (16, 17, 18, 19, 20) *2 times. Work in above-established pat continuing cable pat as on back and maintaining moss st on 12 front border sts, slipping markers on every row. Work until piece measures same as Back to underarm, ending at side edge. Mark row.
Shape Armhole. Next row: Keeping to pat, bind off first 5 (6, 6, 7, 7, 8) sts, finish row. Dec 1 st at armhole edge every other row 6 (6, 7, 7, 8, 8) times—52 (54, 56, 58, 60, 62) sts. Continue in established pat until armhole measures 5¼" (5¼", 5¼", 5½", 5½", 5½") above marked row, ending at front edge.

Shape Neck and Shoulder. Next row: Keeping to pat, bind off first 15 (15, 16, 16, 17, 17) sts, finish row. Dec 1 st at neck edge every other row 10 (11, 11, 12, 12, 13) times and at the same time, when shoulder is same depth as on Back, shape shoulder as on Back. Mark position of 6 buttons evenly spaced on Left Front, with the 1st one 3" (3", 3", 3½", 3½", 3½") from lower edge and the last one ½" below neck edge.

Right Front

With mc and no. 5 needles, co 63 (66, 69, 72, 75, 78) sts. Row 1 (right side): *P 1, k 1* across 1st 12 sts for front border, put a marker on needle, p 15 (16, 17, 18, 19, 20), *k 3, p 15 (16, 17, 18, 19, 20)* 2 times. Continue in above-established pat working to correspond to Left Front, reversing shaping and making buttonholes opposite markers, as follows. Buttonhole row: Keeping to pat, work 5 sts from front edge, bind off next 3 sts, finish row. On next row, work in established pat, casting on 3 sts over bound-off sts.

Sleeves

With mc and no. 5 needles, co 43 (45, 45, 47, 47, 49) sts. Work in moss st for 2". Row 1 (right side): P 2 (2, 1, 1, 0, 0), *k 3, p 15 (16, 17, 18, 19, 20)* 2 times, ending k 3, p 2 (2, 1, 1, 0, 0). Work in above-established pat, continuing cable pat as on Back, inc 1 st each edge every 4th row 16 (17, 18, 19, 21, 22) times working added sts into pat—75 (79, 81, 85, 89, 93) sts. Work even until Sleeve measures 16½" from beg or desired length to underarm.
Shape Cap: Keeping to pat, bind off 5 (6, 6, 7, 7, 8) sts at beg of next 2 rows. Dec 1 st each edge every other row 20 (21, 22, 23, 24, 25) times. Bind off rem 25 (25, 25, 25, 27, 27) sts.

Finishing

Sew shoulder, side and sleeve seams. Sew in Sleeves. Sew on buttons.

To crochet edging

Row 1: From right side, with cc and no. 3 crochet hook, starting at right underarm seam, work 1 row sc along Right Front lower edge, up Right Front, around neck and down Left Front and along remainder of lower edge working 3 sc in each corner. Break off yarn.
Row 2: Join cc at Right Front neck edge. Work *3 sc, ch 4, 1 sc in last sc* along neck edge only. Fasten off.

To embroider

Use needlepoint-crewel yarns and yarn needle. Beg 18" from lower edge on 2nd p panel on Right Front, embroider design following stitches and colors in Embroidered Sweater Pattern 1. Beg 11" from lower edge on 1st p panel on Right Front, embroider design in Embroidered Sweater Pattern 2, following stitches and colors. Embroider Left Front in same manner, reversing designs.

Banners and Flowers

When you're looking for a quick and easy way to make party decorations — or something to keep the children busy on a rainy day — or just a colorful way to brighten up a room — these bold yet simple felt banners and their matching crepe-paper flowers are an excellent solution.

Choose the warm oranges and reds that we used if you're looking for a spicy, south-of-the-border accent, or look to the cooler blues, greens and violets in combination. Or coordinate the banner colors to match your room. White glue does the work; the only stitching you'll do is for the casing and the optional hem. Then hang the banner with fishline or twine.

Make the flowers in a rainbow of colors or as a monochromatic bouquet. Fill a vase with them for a centerpiece or a cocktail-table decoration. Wear a small one in your hair or as a corsage. Make them into napkin holders by wrapping the napkins with the flowers' wire stems. All you need to make the flowers is crepe paper, scissors and wire.

Nearly all the materials you'll need are available in larger variety stores.

BANNER INSTRUCTIONS

You need to make 1 banner

- 2¼ yds. 36"-wide felt in desired color (for design)
- Cardboard (optional)
- Pencil
- Ruler (optional)
- Scissors
- Floor-to-ceiling measure plus 1', or desired length of 36"-wide felt or burlap in contrasting color (for background)
- White glue
- Thread to match felt
- Mat knife (optional)
- 40" long 1" round (dowel rod)
- 44" piece of clear fishing line, heavy string or twine
- Picture-hanging hook

To make inverted-spear banner

1. Cut 2¼ yds. felt into 9 pieces, each to size shown in Fig. 1. Fold each piece in half lengthwise (Fig. 2) and cut off corners as shown in Fig. 3.

2. Center 1st spear on floor-to-ceiling piece and with pencil, mark position of corners. With white glue, glue spear in position. Working in both directions, continue to glue spears to background, leaving 1" between spears and 1" on sides of spears (Fig. 4)

3. Fold 3" under on 1 end of banner and stitch in place for casing. If desired, turn under 1½" on other end of banner for hem; stitch in place. If no hem is desired, trim away at 1½".

4. With mat knife, cut ¼"-deep groove in each end of 1" round ¼" from end; cut groove wide enough to hold fishing line. Tie fishing line to ends so line fits in groove. Hang banner with picture-hanging hook from ceiling or wall.

To make triangle banner

1. With cardboard, ruler and pencil make triangle pattern as in Fig. 5.

2. Cut 21 triangles from felt.

3. Center a triangle on floor-to-ceiling piece and mark location with pencil dots. With white glue, glue triangle in position. Working by rows, continue glueing triangles to background, positioning triangles as in Fig. 6.

4. Finish banner as in steps 3-4 of Inverted-Spear Banner Instructions.

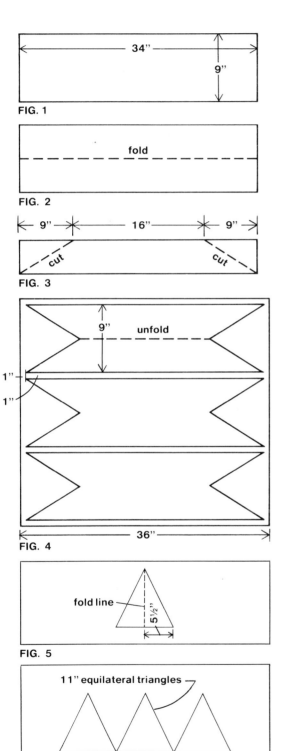

FIG. 1

fold

FIG. 2

9"   16"   9"

cut   cut

FIG. 3

9"   unfold

1"

1"

36"

FIG. 4

fold line   5½"

FIG. 5

11" equilateral triangles

FIG. 6

PAPER FLOWERS INSTRUCTIONS

Each large flower requires three 8" x 18" pieces of crepe paper; each medium flower requires three 6" x 15½" pieces; each small flower requires three 4" x 12" pieces.

You need

- Crepe paper in same or contrasting color(s) as banner(s)
- #7 florist's stem wire cut to 14" lengths

To make

1. Cut crepe paper to desired sizes.

2. Layer 3 identical pieces as in Fig. 7. Fold accordion-style to make about 5 pleats (Fig. 8). Pinch in center and wrap 1 end of wire around center (Fig. 9). Pull layers up and down toward the center to make petals, distributing layers to make even, rounded flower (Fig. 10).

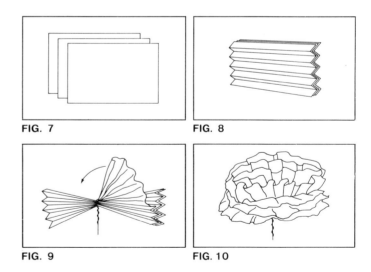

FIG. 7   FIG. 8

FIG. 9   FIG. 10

Smock Sweater

The quick-knitting smock with ribbed yoke is the shape to take you warmly through winter. Knit it with two strands, a fleece/Shetland and a mohair/acrylic. The texture is delicious!

Work sweater using 2 strands, 1 of each yarn, held together throughout.

INSTRUCTIONS

Sizes

Instructions are for size 32 with changes for sizes 34, 36 and 38 in (   ).

Finished measurements

Bustline = 34" (36", 38", 40")
Back at underarm = 17" (19", 19", 20")
Sleeve at underarm = 7" (7¼", 7½", 7¾")

Gauge

3 sts = 1"
4 rows = 1"

You need

- 3 (3, 4, 4) 2-oz. balls 2-ply 95% virgin fleece wool/5% imported Shetland wool in desired color
- 5 (5, 6, 6) 1-oz. balls 2-ply 50% mohair/50% acrylic in same color
- Nos. 11 and 10½ knitting needles
- No. 9 circular 16" knitting needle
- Stitch holder
- Blunt yarn needle

To make

1. Back. With both strands of yarn and no. 11 needles, co 59 (63, 67, 71) sts. Work even in seed st for 5 rows. Row 6: (right side) K 1, p 1, k 1, p 53 (57, 61, 65), k 1, p 1, k 1. Row 7: K 1, p 1, k 55 (59, 63, 67), p 1, k 1. Repeat these 2 rows for pat until piece measures 10" (10½", 11", 11½"). Work even in reverse stockinette st until piece measures 12" (12½", 13", 13½"). Shape Armholes. At beg of next 2 rows bind off 3 sts—53 (57, 61, 65)

sts. Yoke. Change to no. 10½ needles. Row 1: (right side) K 1, *p 3, k 1* across. Row 2: P 1, *k 3, p 1* across. Repeat these 2 rows until ribbing measures 3" (3", 3½", 3½"). 1st dec row: K 1, *p 3, k 1, p 1, p 2 tog* across. Work even until ribbing measures 5" (5", 5½", 5½"). 2nd dec row: K 1, *p 1, p 2 tog, k 1, p 2, k 1* across. Work even until ribbing measures 8" (8", 8½", 8½"). 3rd dec row: K 1, *p 2, k 1, p 2 tog, k 1* across. Work even until ribbing measures 9" (9", 10", 10"). 4th dec row: K 1, *p 2 tog, k 1, p 1, k 1* across. Work even until ribbing measures 9½" (9½", 10½", 10½"). Sl rem 26 (28, 30, 32) sts onto holder.

2. Front. Work same as Back, shaping armholes. Sl rem 53 (57, 61, 65) sts onto holder.

3. Sleeves. With no. 11 needles, co 49 (53, 57, 61) sts and work seed st for 5 rows. Work in reverse stockinette st for 7" (7½", 7½", 7¾"). Shape Cap. At beg of next 2 rows bind off 3 sts, sl rem 43 (47, 51, 55) sts onto holder. Yoke. With right sides facing, sl sts of left sleeve, front and right sleeve onto no. 10½ needles—139 (151, 163, 175) sts. Join yarn at left sleeve edge. Row 1: (right side) P 3, *k 1, p 3* across. Row 2: K 3, *p 1, k 3* across. Repeat these 2 rows for ribbing pat and work all dec rows in same manner as for Back until ribbing measures 9½" (9½", 10½", 10½").

4. Neckband. With no. 9 circular needle, work across in established k 1, p 1 rib the 68 (74, 80, 86) sts of front yoke and 26 (28, 30, 32) sts of back yoke. Join and work 4 rows. Bind off all sts in ribbing.

5. Finishing. Thread yarn needle with single strand of either yarn. Sew underarm, yoke and sleeve seams, leaving open at seed st borders for side slits.

Machine-Embroidered Chair

Machine embroidery is simply fine stitchery done on a sewing machine. It takes much less time than conventional embroidery, and the variety of stitch possibilities is limited only by the capabilities of your particular sewing machine. Many machines have cams or settings for decorative stitching, yet machine embroidery can also be done on a simple portable zigzag machine. For interesting effects try combining zigzag stitches of different lengths and widths with straight stitching.

Each of the nine geometric designs shown on this canvas director's chair is stitched on a separate square through four layers of fabric and interfacing to give it a sturdy quilted effect. Join the squares with strips of fabric, and add quarter-inch dowel rods to the seat to fit the chair's construction. It's a great way to rejuvenate an old chair or perk up a new one.

Experiment with many combinations of arcs, angles and colors. You'll delight in the kaleidoscopic effect as you change stitches and colors and your designs begin to take shape. By decreasing the density of the stitches you can easily use these or any designs on smaller pieces such as placemats, napkin holders, shirts or blouses and eyeglass cases.

INSTRUCTIONS

You need

- Machine Embroidery Patterns (page 201)
- ⅝ yd. 45"-wide cocoa 100%-cotton fabric
- 1 yd. 40"-wide fleece nonwoven interfacing
- Enlarging Patterns materials (see page 206)
- Transferring Patterns materials (see page 206)
- Cotton or polyester thread in a variety of colors
- ¾ yd. 45"-wide suntan 100%-cotton fabric
- Cotton or polyester suntan thread
- Two ¼" dowel rods, each 15" long
- Zipper foot
- Latex satin-finish enamel paint in desired color
- Standard-size director's chair
- Paintbrush

To make

All seam allowances = ½" unless otherwise indicated. Clean, oil and lubricate sewing machine before beginning. Do not over-oil. Continually check machine for lint and clean accordingly.

Cam machines

Select desired cam and place in machine. Use size 16 or 18 needle. Thread machine. With fabric scraps, sandwich 1 or 2 layers of

interfacing between 2 layers of cotton and stitch through all layers with desired decorative stitch to test tension. Adjust tension. Follow this procedure each time you change cam.

1. Cut eighteen 6½" squares each from cocoa fabric and interfacing. Sandwich 2 interfacing squares between 2 cotton squares. With properly adjusted machine baste together cotton and interfacing along edges. Repeat for all squares.

2. With Enlarging Patterns Materials, bring desired Patterns in Machine Embroidery Patterns up to full size. With Transferring Patterns Materials, trace on padded squares, or with dressmaker's pencil lightly mark basic lines of desired full-size pattern on padded squares. Machine embroider desired design along lines on each square using decorative stitches; leave ⅝" along each edge free of decorative stitching. Embellish designs within lines as desired. After machine embroidery is complete, join squares together in 3 panels of 3 by zigzagging as in Fig. 1.

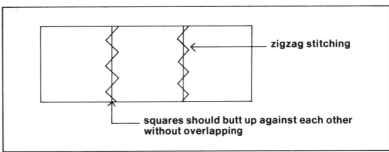

FIG. 1

3. Cut suntan fabric into the following pieces along crosswise grain: twelve 2" x 6½" strips; four 2" x 20" strips; two 5" x 20" strips; two 5" x 17" strips; four 5" x 8" rectangles.

4. On each 2" x 6½" strip, fold ½" to wrong side along each long edge; press. Place 1 pressed strip over each zigzagged seam, covering ½" seam allowance on each square. Pin in place, turn over and pin pressed strip to back in same manner. Zigzag strips to squares along strip edges. Make 2 panels for chair seat and 1 for chair back.

5. On two 2" x 20" strips, fold ½" to wrong side along each long edge; press. With 1 strip on top and 1 on bottom, stitch 2 panels together lengthwise as in step 4. On remaining 2" x 20" strips, fold ¼" to wrong side; press. Fold in half with wrong sides together; press. Zigzag strips to long edges of remaining 3-square panel for chair back.

6. Finishing long edges of seat. Fold ½" to wrong side along each long edge of 5" x 20" strips; press. Cut two 4" x 20" strips of interfacing; pin 1 to wrong side of each 5" x 20" strip between folds. Fold faced strips in half lengthwise; press. Encase each long edge in folded strip by placing folds ½" from edge and zigzagging along folds through all layers. Set machine for straight stitching, topstitch strip ¼" from each long edge, then topstitch in zigzag pattern between the 2 stitching lines (see photograph).

7. Finishing short edges of seat. Fold one 5" x 17" strip in half lengthwise with right sides together, stitch across each end in ½" seam allowance; turn to right side. Length of strip should equal short edge of chair seat. Fold ½" to wrong side along long strip edges; press. Insert 1 dowel rod in strip and push against fold. With zipper foot, stitch close to dowel along full length of strip. Encase seat edge in strip by placing folds ½" from edge and zigzagging along folds through all layers. Reinforce with 2 rows of straight stitching along length of strip next to zigzag stitching. Repeat on remaining edge.

8. Finishing short edges of back. Zigzag short edge of back to prevent raveling. Cut one 5" x 8" interfacing rectangle. Stitch to wrong side of one 5" x 8" cotton rectangle. With right sides together, stitch faced rectangle to 1 cotton rectangle along edges, leaving 3" opening along one 8" edge. Clip across corners; turn to right side; fold seam allowance at opening to inside; press. Fold in half lengthwise and pin to short edge of back so rectangle edges are ½" from back edge. Zigzag through all layers along rectangle edges. Repeat on remaining edge.

9. Paint chair frame; let dry. Leave frame slightly folded with arms down; slide dowel edges of seat into chair grooves; bring arms up; slide chair back onto spindles at back of chair; open chair completely so fabric is taut. ○

Mola

This colorful textile art is essentially a combination of multi-level reverse appliqué and standard appliqué. A beautiful design is achieved as layers of fabric in different colors are cut away to reveal a shape in a new color. Then successively smaller replacement layers are appliquéd on. The end result is a bright design in which color surrounds color.

The Cuna Indians of the San Blas Islands off the northern coast of Panama invented the mola. The original motifs used by the Cuna women were taken from everyday life, mythology or the Spanish conquistadores—who were never able to conquer or subjugate the Cunas. Most of the earliest pieces have been lost; molas are used by the Cuna to decorate blouses and Cuna women were always buried in their best blouses.

In a basic mola, from three to seven (usually five) different-colored fabrics are stacked one upon the next and randomly basted to hold them in place as the design is brought forth. The "mola look" comes into its own as portions of the first fabric layer are cut away, revealing the color of the second layer. The same cutting-away process is applied to expose all existing layers; in our mola, sections of the bottom layer have been replaced with still more colors.

Make two identical molas and use them in a blouse as the Cunas do, or make one mola, mount it and display it proudly on your wall.

MOLA INSTRUCTIONS

You need

- Mola Patterns (pages 202-203)
- Enlarging Patterns materials (see page 206)
- Lightweight 45"-wide cotton without permanent press finish as follows:
    ½ yd. red
    ⅜ yd. yellow
    ⅜ yd. black
    ⅛ yd. each (or scraps) white, blue, lavender, orange, pink, green
- Transferring Patterns materials (see page 206)
- Sharp dressmaker's pencil
- Thread to match each color

To make

Change thread as you go to match fabric you are working on. Press only when necessary.

1. Cut red, yellow and black cotton into one 18" x 22" rectangle each. Reserve remnants.

2. With Enlarging Patterns Materials, bring Mola Pattern 1 up to full size. Fold tracing paper and draw design again on remaining half.

3. With Transferring Patterns Materials, transfer solid lines of design to red fabric. Reinforce design on fabric with a line made with sharp dressmaker's pencil.

4. Stack 1 black, 1 yellow and the red traced rectangle in that order with red on top. Pin together. Hand baste through all layers at random locations between lines of design and around edge of stack to prevent slippage.

5. Following the lines on the red fabric, cut, fold and stitch by this method: Beginning at any point along cutting line, cut along line 1"-3", fold under ⅛" seam allowance toward outside edge of rectangle, stitch fold to yellow layer beneath it with small whipstitches. Clip almost to fold where necessary to keep curves smooth and corners square. Roll up and pin portion of panel you are not working on to assure that pencil marks will not rub away. Reserve the red cutouts; they will be applied later as an appliquéd replacement layer.

6. When all red folds are stitched in place, yellow will appear inside lines of design. Cut, fold and stitch as in step 5, cutting ⅛" in from red folds so that ⅛" yellow will show along red folds when work on yellow layer is complete. (Broken lines on Pat. 1 show cutting line for yellow.) Cut only the yellow layer. Black will appear inside lines of design. If desired, reserve yellow cutouts for later use as replacement layer.

7. With Enlarging Patterns Materials, bring Mola Pattern 2 up to full size. Replace the cut-out yellow layer with 1-4 layers in other shades with the following method: Using Pat. 2 and colors denoted there, cut 1st replacement layer for bird and dog. Fold each layer under ⅛" and whipstitch to bird and dog. For flower, use Pat. 1, cutting 1st replacement layer ⅛" smaller than Pattern.

8. Using colors listed below, cut each successive replacement layer ⅛" smaller than preceding one, fold under ⅛" and whipstitch to mola.

> Bird: neck — red; wing — white, red; underbody — white, red.
> Dog: head — white, red; tail — red; body — red.

9. To hem panel, turn under ¾" on all 4 sides and baste close to fold. (Basting will be removed after stitching panel to frame.)

MOLA MOUNTING INSTRUCTIONS

You need

- Two 22" canvas stretchers
- Two 28" canvas stretchers
- 4 Scotch fasteners
- ¾ yd. 36"- or 45"-wide black cotton
- Staple gun or short carpet tacks and hammer
- 2 screw eyes and picture-hanging wire
- One 16½" x 20½" mola panel

To make

Assemble canvas stretchers, reinforcing corners with Scotch fasteners. Stretch black cotton fabric over frame and fasten <u>from back of frame</u> with staples or tacks. Begin fastening at center of each stretcher and work toward corners (see Fig. 1). Alternate working on each side for even tension and straight grain; do not finish one side at a time. Fasten screw eyes and wire to back just above center. Center mola panel on fabric frame and stitch in place by hand.

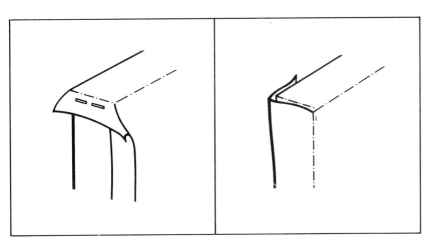

FIG. 1
TURNING CORNERS ON STRETCHER FRAME

Caftan

Besides being one of the most comfortable and versatile modes of dress ever devised, the caftan is also one of the easiest to sew. This caftan is made with a self-capelet that drapes over your back for a truly romantic look. Make it to fit your own measurements and cut the curves that form the capelet edges with a pie plate. Stitch it up on the sewing machine, step in and pull the capelet over your head, and that's it! Stitch up a few in a variety of fabrics for all-day dressing.

INSTRUCTIONS

Sizes

Instructions are for size 10-12. Caftan should fit loosely around hips. To increase size, use 54"- or 60"-wide fabric in a longer yardage. Cut to fit and adjust seam allowances and hem. To decrease size, cut fabric to fit.

You need

- 2 yds. 48"-wide cotton print fabric
- Thread to match
- 1"-wide bias tape to match
- ½ yd. ½"-wide elastic

To make

1. Place fabric flat on work surface. Cut rounded end, 12" slits and neck hole (Fig. 1). Stitch ½" hem along rounded edge, slits and neck hole edge.

2. Stitch edges together for back seam in ½" seam allowance, leaving 20" at bottom for slit. Stitch bias tape in place to wrong side at top edge for casing (Fig. 2). Draw elastic through casing and pin in place at each end of casing, allowing about 15" of elastic between pins. Step into caftan and slip head through hole. (Fig. 3); adjust elastic and determine finished length of caftan. Stitch elastic to caftan at casing ends and trim away excess elastic. Machine hem 20" slit edges and bottom edge of caftan.

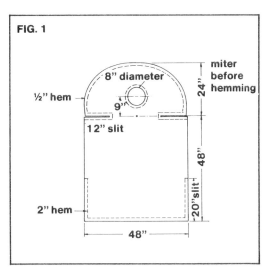

FIG. 1

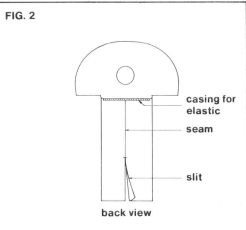

FIG. 2

casing for elastic

seam

slit

back view

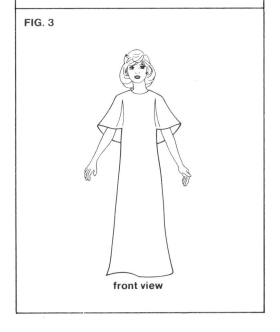

FIG. 3

front view

Crochet Eggs

Dress your eggs in a fresh wardrobe of crochet cotton and beads this Easter. It's a colorful and refreshing change from colored dyes or paints. And these eggs are so beautiful you'll want to display them Easter after Easter — or all during the year.

Start by carefully blowing out the contents of a raw egg. Wrap the empty shell in a solid color of yarn; then decorate it in contrasting colors with beads, tiny crocheted motifs or free-form yarn.

INSTRUCTIONS

You need

- Sharp needle
- Raw eggs
- Masking tape
- Crochet cotton in a variety of colors and sizes
- ¼" flat artist's paintbrush
- White glue
- Small pointed artist's paintbrush
- Plastic beads (optional)
- No. 7 steel crochet hook

To make

1. Blow out contents of eggs as follows: With needle, poke small hole in 1 end of egg, moving needle around inside of egg to break up membrane. Make 1 hole slightly larger at other end and blow through smaller hole until inside of egg is forced out through larger hole. Rinse and dry eggshell. Place small square of masking tape over each hole.

2. Select desired color of crochet cotton. With ¼" paintbrush, apply glue to 1 end of egg; place end of cotton on center of glued area and wrap cotton around (see photograph). Apply glue to next ¼" of egg and continue wrapping crochet cotton. Cover entire egg by this method. Cut off cotton when finished; glue end in place.

3. Determine designs and placement of designs on eggs. Use crochet cotton and crochet hook.

Glued designs

(See yellow, orange and pink egg in photograph.) With pointed paintbrush, apply glue to covered egg where designs will be placed. Put designs and/or beads over glue, pushing gently in place.

Crochet motif 1

(See pink and green floral egg in photograph.) Starting at center, ch 6, join with sl st to form ring. Rnd 1: Ch 3 (counts as 1 dc), dc 15 in ring, join with sl st to 3rd st of ch-3 first made. Fasten off.

Crochet motif 2

(See blue and lavender egg in photograph.) Work as for Motif 1; do not fasten off. Rnd 2: *Ch 5, sk 1 dc, sc in next dc* around (8 loops made). Rnd 3: *Sc, hdc, 3 dc, hdc, sc* in 1st loop, repeat in rem 7 loops, sl st in 1st sc. Fasten off.

Crochet motif 3

(See light and dark green egg in photograph.) Starting at center, ch 6, join with sl st to form ring. *Sc 1, ch 5* in ring 8 times. Fasten off. ○

Woven Rya Pillows

Rya weaving is a Scandinavian technique noted for its beauty and durability. The word rya originally referred to the knot used to tie strands of yarn to the inside of bed clothing for added warmth during long Scandinavian winters. Today the word can refer to many things—the luscious and lustrous, yet strong, yarn, the knot itself or the whole piece that results.

Accessorize a couch or bed with rough-and-tumble pillows made of sturdy rya yarn that you've woven into fabric accented with shaggy rya knots. If you've never woven before, with inexpensive weaving wool practice warping your loom and weaving small pieces before you begin this project.

Rya wool is available in most stores that sell weaving supplies. If the weaving is tight and the stuffing can be dry cleaned, the pillows need no lining.

INSTRUCTIONS

You need

- Loom that weaves a 16" width, with shuttle
- Three 110-yd. skeins 2-ply rya weaving wool (for warp and weft)
- Scraps of heavy yarn
- 110 yds. 2-ply rya weaving wool in assorted colors (for rya pile)
- Yarn needle
- 1 bag polyester fiber stuffing

To set up loom

With rya weaving wool, warp loom for 16" width. Approximately 1" will be taken up in weaving and another inch will be taken up in seam allowances. Set up the loom in a straight draw with sheds alternating warp movement up and down, and with 2 threads on each side treated as 1 for selvages. One shed will control threads 1 (actually 2 threads), 3, 5, etc., and the other shed will control threads 2, 4, 6, etc. Straight draw results in a plain weave.

To make pillows

1. Heading. With scraps of heavy yarn, plain weave 4 rows. Heading keeps warp yarns evenly spaced; later it will be removed.

2. With rya weaving wool, plain weave for 5".

3. Rya pile. Place both harnesses at rest. Cut assorted colors of rya wool in 6"-8" pieces, varying the lengths. Begin pile 3½" from selvage and a few inches above previous weaving by laying 4-8 precut yarn pieces on top of 2 warp threads. Wrap the cut pieces around the 2 warp threads; bring ends up between the warp threads and pull up (Fig. 1). Pull completed knot toward you so it rests against weaving. Skip a warp thread. Repeat rya knot procedure on the next 2 warp threads. Continue knotting and skipping a thread across the loom until you are 3½" from selvage. Beat down row of knots with beater bar. Plain weave 4 rows (4 passages of shuttle). Repeat rya knot and plain weave pattern for 5".

4. Plain weave for 20". This completes front and back of pillow.

5. Cut woven fabric from loom by cutting across warp threads about 5" from last row of weaving and about 4" from heading. Remove heading from bottom of fabric. Tie overhand knots in groups of 4 as close to weaving as possible to secure. Trim knot ends to 2".

6. Fold rectangle in half, right sides together. Pile should be centered on pillow front. With yarn needle and same wool used in weaving, sew 2 selvage edges together in ¼" seam; turn right sides out. Stuff with polyester fiber and sew open side closed, tucking fringe and turning in ¼" seam allowance as you stitch. ○

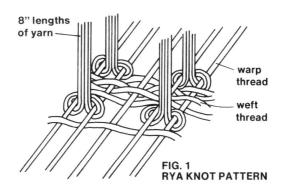

8" lengths of yarn

warp thread

weft thread

**FIG. 1
RYA KNOT PATTERN**

Canvas Plants

For a spritely contrast to the green, leafy and live variety of plants, stitch up a canvas mother-in-law's tongue or cactus. Make a grouping and arrange them in terra cotta pots—these plants never need watering or misting and they're sure to live long and decorative lives. Even if you have a "purple thumb," you'll manage your canvas plants beautifully!

Build the mother-in-law's tongue on part of a wire coat hanger and support it in styrofoam. Stuff the cactus with polyester batting and support it with crushed tissue paper. White gravel, available at florist- and aquarium-supply stores, makes everything look lifelike.

MOTHER-IN-LAW'S TONGUE INSTRUCTIONS

You need
- Plant Pattern 1 (page 204)
- 5" x 26" piece of cardboard or paper
- Enlarging Patterns materials (see page 206)
- 1 yd. 50"-wide natural-colored heavyweight canvas
- Heavy-duty thread to match canvas
- #16 sewing machine needle
- Wire cutters
- 8 wire coat hangers
- 9" x 16" sheet of 1"-thick styrofoam
- .8" clay flowerpot with liner
- White gravel

To make

1. With Enlarging Patterns Materials, bring Plant Pattern 1 up to full size. Cut 16 leaf pieces.

2. With right sides together, stitch 2 leaf pieces together along curved edges in ¼" seam. Reinforce stitching at point; trim seam allowance to ⅛" at point and turn to right side. Press gently. Repeat to make 8 leaves total.

3. With wire cutters, snip off hook portion of wire coat hanger. Straighten wire; make small loop in 1 end. Insert wire in leaf with loop at point. Clip off wire 2" below bottom edge of leaf (Pat. 1). Fold along wire at bottom edge; whipstitch closed.

4. Cut 2 circles of styrofoam so they will wedge into clay pot about 1" from top. Insert wire ends of leaves into center of styrofoam as in photograph. Bend leaves to desired angles. Spread gravel over styrofoam.

CACTUS INSTRUCTIONS

You need

- Plant Pattern 2 (page 204)
- 99" x 50" piece of cardboard or paper
- Enlarging Patterns materials (see page 206)
- 2 ¾ yds. 50" wide natural-colored heavyweight canvas
- Heavy-duty thread to match canvas
- #16 sewing machine needle
- 35' heavy string
- Large-eyed sharp needle
- 1 package polyester batting
- 3 packages white tissue wrapping paper
- Three 12" clay flowerpots with liners
- White gravel

To make

1. With cardboard and Enlarging Patterns Materials, bring Plant Pattern 2 up to full size. Cut 6 pieces for each length (30", 40" and 50") from canvas (Fig. 1).

2. Assembling. Fold 1 cactus section in half lengthwise with right sides together, matching curved cut edge above fold. Stitch in ¼" seam along folded edge (Fig. 2A). Repeat with 2nd section. With right sides together, join the 2 stitched sections along 1 curved edge in ¼" seam (Fig. 2B). Encase seam allowance to form French seam ridge by folding sections along stitching with wrong sides together and topstitching ½" from fold on right side (Fig. 2C). Continue procedure with 1 section at a time until all sections are connected to form a cylinder. At top where seams come together, pull raw edges to inside and whipstitch ridges together, 2 at a time.

3. Adding string tufts. Thread needle with 2'-3' string. Push needle through ridge near edge; pull string through, leaving about a 3" end. Tie knot and trim string 1½" from knot to make tuft. Tie 1 tuft approximately every 8" along ridge, alternating tuft positions on next ridge so tufts are staggered (see photograph).

4. Stuffing cactus. Roll batting until diameter easily fits into cactus; slide roll into cactus. Trim off excess batting at bottom. With crushed tissue paper, stuff bottom of clay pot firmly to depth of 3". Place cactus on tissue in center of pot; stuff crushed tissue around cactus to within 1" of top until firm enough to support cactus without puckering canvas. Spread gravel on tissue around cactus.

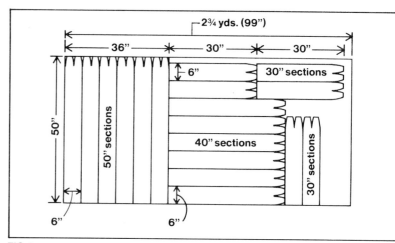

FIG. 1
CACTUS LAYOUT

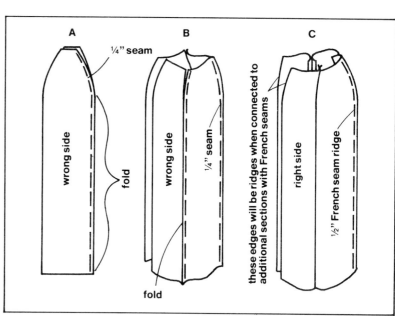

FIG. 2
ASSEMBLING CACTUS

Crochet Lion Pillow

Create this warm and friendly fellow with an unusual yet easy crochet technique. Work half double crochet or double crochet into spaces in the previous row, rather than under two threads. You'll achieve an overall nubby texture that's especially interesting. If you don't follow the stitch count exactly, that's all right, too — a bit of unevenness adds an extra bit of life to this shaggy-maned lion.

INSTRUCTIONS

Gauge
5 sts = 2"
6 rows = 2"

You need
- 4-ply knitting worsted as follows:
    - 3 oz. light orange (A)
    - 6 oz. red (B)
    - 3 oz. green (C)
    - 3 oz. purple (D)
    - 3 oz. bright orange (E)
    - 3 oz. turquoise (F)
- Size K crochet hook
- 2 bobby pins
- Large-eyed yarn needle
- ½ yd. lining fabric
- 6 oz. polyester fiber stuffing
- 7"-wide thick cardboard

To make

Work hdc in spaces rather than into stitches for a nubbier texture. Work Face from bottom up. Work Nose, Eyes and Eye Pouches separately, then add to face. Work Back separately, then stitch to Face. Hook on strands of Mane.

Mouth

Row 1: With A, ch 3, turn and hdc in 2nd st from hook and rem st, ch 1, turn. Row 2: Work hdc in each sp of previous row, ch 1, turn. Row 3: Work hdc across, inc 1 st at bcg and cnd of row, ch 1, turn. Row 4: Work hdc in 6 sps, ch 1, turn. Rows 5-8: Repeat row 3. Row 9: Work hdc in 14 sps, ch1, turn. Row 10: Work hdc in 7 sps, ch 1, turn. Rows 11-12: Work hdc across 7 sts, dec 1 st at beg of each row, sl st in last st, fasten off after sl st in row 12.

Forming heart-shaped piece. Attach yarn in 8th st of row 9. Repeat rows 10-12.

Face

Row 1: Attach B at outside edge of Mouth in 3rd row from top (wide end), ch 1 and work 3 hdc in each row working up toward top edge, hdc across top of Mouth, hdc in each of 3 rows working down toward bottom of Mouth, ch 1, turn (approx 18 sts). Row 2: Work hdc in each sp of previous row, inc 1 at beg and end of row, ch 1, turn. Row 3: Work hdc across, ch 1, turn. Rows 4-5: Repeat row 2. Rows 6-7: Work hdc across, ch 1, turn. Row 8: Repeat row 2. Rows 9-11: Work hdc across, ch 1, turn. Row 12: Repeat row 2. Rows 13-22: Work hdc across (approx 28 sts), ch 1, turn. Rows 23-30: Work hdc across, dec 1 at beg and end of each row, ch 1, turn, fasten off at end of row 30.

"Smile" line

Attach C in outside st of 3rd row from top of Mouth and sc in sps of Mouth piece to make smooth curve to "V" of Mouth, and then to outside st of 3rd row on other side of Mouth.

Mouth border

Attach color A in center "V" of Mouth, ch 1, hdc around edge of Mouth, adding extra stitches at chin (narrow end) for smooth curve. Fasten off.

Nose

Row 1: With B, ch 5, turn; beg with 2nd st from hook, hdc in 4 sts, ch 1, turn. Rows 2-6: Work hdc across, ch 1, turn. Rows 7-8: Work hdc across, inc 1 at beg of each row, ch 1, turn. Rows 9-10: Work hdc across, ch 1, turn, fasten off at end of row 10. Rows 11-12: Attach C, hdc across, fasten off at end of row 12. Rows 13-14: Attach C in 2nd st from end, ch 1, hdc in next 2 sps, ch 1, turn, hdc in 2 sps, fasten off at end of row 14.

Nose accent

Attach C in row 11, hdc across these 6 sps, fasten off.

Nose trim

Attach C in upper left-hand top of Nose, hdc around Nose, inc where needed to make smooth curves. Fasten off. Center Nose on Face (see photograph) and secure with 2 bobby pins at top and bottom. With C and yarn needle, sew Nose to Face along trim row. With B sew top of Nose (4 sts) to Face.

Eye border

Make 2.

With C, hook through top trim st of Nose and corresponding Face st, knot. Pull loose end to back of work. Sc diagonally up 2, across 4, down 4, across 4, diagonally up 2 to form oval-like circle. Fasten off and fasten to other end at back.

Eyes

Half spheres worked in rnds. Make 2.

Rnd 1: With D, ch 3, sl st to form circle, ch 1, work 6 hdc in center of circle, join, ch 1. Rnd 2: Work hdc around, inc 1 at beg and end of rnd, join, ch 1. Rnd 3: Work hdc around, inc 1 at end of rnd, join, fasten off, leaving 12" end. Thread yarn needle with end and sew Eye to Face inside Eye Border.

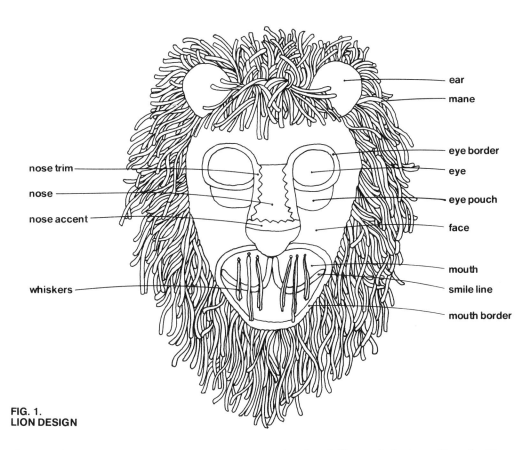

nose trim

nose

nose accent

whiskers

ear

mane

eye border

eye

eye pouch

face

mouth

smile line

mouth border

FIG. 1.
LION DESIGN

Eye pouches

Make 2.

Row 1: With E, ch 5, turn beg with 2nd st from hook, hdc into 4 sts, ch 1, turn. Row 2: Work hdc across, ch 1, turn. Row 3: Work hdc across, dec 1 at beg. Fasten off. Position on Face (see Fig. 1) and with E and yarn needle, sew to Face under Eye.

Whiskers

Cut 6-10 eight-inch strands of D and hook into upper Mouth (see Fig. 1).

Back

Rows 1-8: With B, work first 8 rows of Mouth instructions. Rows 9-12: Work hdc, ch 1, turn. Rows 13-15: Work hdc across, inc 1 at beg and end, ch 1, turn. Tie on marking string here. Rows 16-42: Continue with rows 4-30 of Face instructions.

Ears

Make 2.

With B, ch 6. Work 6 rows hdc, work hdc around Ear and sew to top of front piece.

Mane

Wrap all colors around cardboard. Cut once, leaving 14" strands for long Mane for Face side, bottom and back.

Forehead. Cut 7" strands as needed. In left hand, hold folded strand; with right hand, push hook through a horizontal row st, hook strand loop, pull loop under st, pull ends of strand through loop and gently tighten. Hook 2 separate 7" strands in each sp across top of head, in front of ears and around Face piece down to top of nose.

Sides and back. Using same method, attach 14" strands in Face sides, chin and over entire Back piece. If desired, alternate rows in Back only as follows: 1 row of 2 strands in each sp, then 1 row of 1 strand in each sp. If desired, trim strands around Face and chin.

Lining and assembly

With lion front as pat, cut 2 linings with 2" seam allowance on all edges.

Assembly. Sew lining pieces tog using ½" seam; leave 6" opening at top. Stuff lining; whipstitch opening closed. Place stuffed lining in lion. To close top 6" of lion, tie tog a few strands from front and Back pieces. Untie to remove stuffed lining when lion needs dry cleaning. If desired, create a 3-D effect along seam between front and Back pieces by pulling 1 of the front strands through to back and tying into back Mane at 3" intervals.

Bed Jackets

Soft wools in soft colors knit snuggly warm and oh-so-feminine bed jackets for mother and daughter. The gauge is open and the work goes fast so it's easy to make matching sets in contrasting or identical colors. These jackets easily leave the bedroom, too, when they're worn over a turtleneck or turtle-shirt combination. Crochet chains form the ties.

INSTRUCTIONS

Sizes

Instructions are for children's size small with changes for children's medium and large, misses' small, medium and large in (   ).

Finished measurements

Width of garment at underarms: 27" (29", 31", 32½", 35¾", 39¼")

Gauge

3 sts = 1"
5 rows = 1"

You need

- 5 (5, 6, 9, 10, 10) 40-gram (about 1.4 oz.) balls mohair yarn
- No. 11 knitting needles (or size that will give proper gauge)
- Stitch holder
- No. 0 crochet hook

To make

Entire garment is worked with a double strand of yarn. Garment is worked horizontally from left front to right front. Beg at left front co 42 (45, 48, 72, 72, 72) sts. Row 1 (right side): Knit. Row 2: Knit. Row 3: K 38 (41, 44, 66, 66, 66) sts, turn. Row 4: Sl 1 as if to k, k to end of row. Row 5: K 30 (33, 36, 52, 52, 52), turn. Row 6: Sl 1 as if to k, k to end of row. Repeat rows 1-6 throughout for pat. Work 35 (37, 39, 41, 47, 53) rows. Row 36 (38, 40, 42, 48, 54): K to last 27 (30, 33, 46, 46, 46) sts and sl them onto holder. Next row: Co 27 (30, 33, 46, 46, 46) for sleeve. Continue in pat on all sts as before. Work 46 (52, 58, 64, 70, 76) rows, end wrong side. Next row: Bind off 1st 27 (30, 33, 46, 46, 46) sts, finish row. Turn and work to bound-off sts, pick up and k 27 (30, 33, 46, 46, 46) from holder. Work 65 (71, 75, 77, 83, 89) rows for back. Next row: Work as for row 36 (38, 40, 42, 48, 54). Then work 2nd sleeve like 1st sleeve until 46 (52, 58, 64, 70, 76) rows have been completed. Next row: Bind off 1st 27 (30, 33, 46, 46, 46) sts, finish row. Turn and work to bound-off sts, pick up and k 27 (30, 33, 46, 46, 46) sts from holder. Then work 36 (38, 40, 42, 48, 54) rows for right front. Bind off.

Finishing

Sew underarm seams on sleeves.
Tie: With 4 strands of yarn and crochet hook, ch 25. Cut 2 of the 4 strands; continue with 2 strands around neck by inserting hook into right front corner and work 1 sl st in each ridge around neck until left front corner is reached. Join 2 more strands of yarn to make 4 and ch 25. Fasten off.

Basket Lamps

Bring sophistication back home in lamps made with natural fibers, textures and colors. The naturalness won't overwhelm printed fabrics and provides a pleasant contrast for solids. And on both lamps, a safe yet easy-to-assemble wiring system lets you create the perfect means to light up your life.

The hanging lamp is based on a design from Haiti. Use sisal cord to weave it on a frame made with wire coat hangers or clothesline wire. A fiberglass cylinder shields the bulb and additional sisal conceals the cord. Make the table lamp with a purchased seagrass basket and linen-look shade (or use a basket you made yourself with the instructions on page 91). The light bulb is positioned as close to eye level as possible so light can be spread over the largest area.

HANGING LAMP INSTRUCTIONS

You need

- 11 wire coat hangers or one 25' roll of clothesline wire
- Long-nose pliers
- Lamp frame with 8" diameter and ⅜" center hole
- Wire cutter
- 175 yds. sisal
- 1 yd. heavy string
- 12" x 12" scrap of ½" plywood
- Staple gun
- 17" x 25" piece fiberglass
- 1 medium-size nail
- File
- Hammer
- Clear epoxy glue
- About 1 yd. nylon fish line
- 3½" length of ⅛" I. P. pipe
- 3 brass ring nuts for I. P. pipe
- Pull-chain socket
- 1¾" brass finish loop with ⅛" I. P. female thread
- 16' white electrical cord
- 1 Kwik Cap Leviton Plug
- 100-watt light bulb
- 1 or more swag hooks

To make

1. With pliers, shape a circle of coat-hanger wire same size as lamp frame; hook closed (Fig. 1). Cut ten 25" lengths of coat-hanger wire, bend ends into hooks and attach to lamp frame and circle (Fig. 1). Wrap sisal around lamp frame and circle (Fig. 2). Tie heavy string to center of lamp frame; place shade on plywood and staple string to plywood (Fig. 2) to cause wires to curve and hold shade in place for sisal wrapping.

2. Starting at bottom, wrap sisal around wire shade (Fig. 3) looping sisal around each wire and pulling taut after each loop. Loops should all face inside of shade for smooth exterior. As wires are wrapped, they will take on a natural slant. Remove shade from plywood; remove string from shade.

3. Punch holes along the two 25" edges of fiberglass at 1" intervals as follows: Blunt nail by rubbing on file. Place plywood scrap under fiberglass; position nail ¼" from edge of fiberglass and pound through into plywood with hammer. Form fiberglass into a cylinder with holes at top and bottom. Overlap ends about ½"; adjust size to fit through wire circle. Staple overlap at top and bottom and tie 2-3 pieces of string around cylinder to hold. Trim away excess over ½" overlap, if necessary. Glue overlap with clear epoxy glue; let set. Remove staples and strings. Slide cylinder into shade and with fish line, lace cylinder to top and bottom edges of shade through holes.

4. Wiring Lamp. Screw 1 brass ring nut on each end of I. P. pipe. Screw socket at bottom end and tighten lower ring nut against it. Tighten socket screw. Slide pipe up through lamp-frame bracket and screw 3rd ring nut onto pipe above bracket. Tighten ring nuts against bracket, allowing ¼" of pipe to extend above bracket. Screw threaded loop onto extended pipe (Fig. 4).

5. Feed electrical cord through loop and pipe and connect to socket as follows: Strip insulation ½" from end of cord; pull off socket cover and thread wire through socket neck. Make a loop knot with strands about 1" from stripped end. Twist exposed wire strands and wrap 1 wire clockwise around each terminal. Screw terminals tight and push socket parts together.

6. Attach plug to other end of cord. Wrap or knot sisal around cord for finished look. Screw light bulb in place. With swag hooks, hang from ceiling.

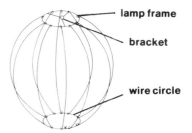

FIG. 1
WIRE SHADE FRAME

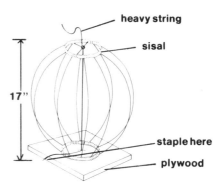

FIG. 2
ANCHORING SHADE FRAME

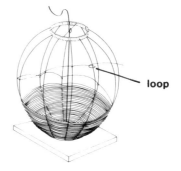

FIG.3
WRAPPING SISAL

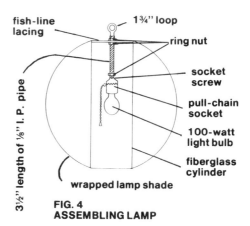

FIG. 4
ASSEMBLING LAMP

TABLE LAMP INSTRUCTIONS

You need

- ¼"-thick plywood square to fit inside bottom of basket
- 12"-high basket
- Two ⅛" ring nuts
- 13¼" length of threaded ⅛" I. P. pipe
- 5" cast-iron loader with groove for electrical cord
- 12¼" length of ¼" brass tubing
- Square of burlap 2" larger than plywood
- 8' length of gold electrical cord with molded plug
- 9" lamp harp
- 3-way socket
- Paste epoxy glue
- Clear epoxy glue
- White glue
- 100-watt light bulb
- 10½"-high lampshade
- 1" loop finial

To make

1. Trial assembly. (See Fig. 5.) Insert plywood square in bottom of basket. Screw 1 ring nut onto end of I. P. pipe. Screw end of pipe into smooth upper side of loader so pipe is flush with underside of loader. Tighten ring nut against loader. Slide brass tubing over pipe. Push threads apart at center of burlap square and slide over tubing down to loader. Screw on 2nd ring nut against top of brass tubing. (Cut off excess brass tubing if insufficient length of pipe is exposed for fastening harp and socket.) Push straw apart at bottom edge of basket along 1 side to make hole for electrical cord. Place loader-pipe assembly in bottom of basket on top of plywood square. Thread non-plug end of cord through hole in basket, along groove in loader and up pipe.

2. Fasten harp and socket in place, wiring socket as follows: Strip insulation on electrical cord ½" from end of cord. Split the 2 insulated strands of cord about 1½" down from exposed wires. Pull socket apart; thread stripped wires through bottom portion of socket. Make a loop knot with strands about 1" from stripped wires to keep cord from sliding down pipe. Twist exposed wire strands and wrap 1 wire clockwise around each terminal in top portion of socket. Screw terminals tight and push socket parts together.

3. Disassemble lamp by removing loader with pipe, harp and socket attached from plywood base. Remove plywood base from basket.

4. Final assembly. Mix paste epoxy on underside of plywood base. Smear daub of epoxy about the size of thumbnail on each corner and in center of base. Center base in bottom of basket, push firmly in place, weight down base and let set. Disassemble remainder of lamp, leaving socket wiring in place. Reassemble lamp, reinforcing each joint with daub of clear epoxy. When clear epoxy is set, mix paste epoxy on underside of loader. Smear epoxy evenly around edge of loader and place daub in groove to hold cord in place. Center loader-pipe assembly on base in basket, making sure the distance from tubing to each basket side is equal. Pull electrical cord taut and firmly press loader in place on base. When centered and straight, weight down and let set overnight. With white glue, fasten burlap in place over loader; apply glue sparingly to perimeter of burlap.

5. Insert bulb in socket. Attach lampshade and loop finial to complete lamp (see Fig. 6). ○

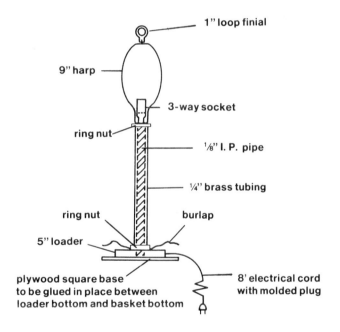

FIG. 5

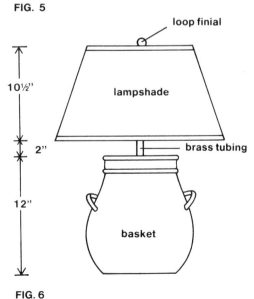

FIG. 6

Paper Sculpture Centerpiece

Adorn a first (paper) wedding anniversary or a fresh-as-dew outdoor brunch on a bright and sunny day with this delicate paper centerpiece. Set on a cardboard base, the centerpiece blossoms into an artful bouquet with gracefully hovering butterflies. Repeat the paper theme with a sculptured napkin ring for each guest.

In the Orient, artists — and nearly everyone else — have known about paper art for centuries. However, much of the Oriental work has been in Japan, with origami, folding paper to make three-dimensional designs, and kirigami, three-dimensional designs made from paper that has been cut as well as folded. Paper sculpture, a more recently developed form, permits fastening with glue, paste or staples in addition to folding and cutting to achieve the design.

Don't try to hurry your paper sculpture into existence. Carefully measure and cut or score each line of each piece. Be sure a section is securely fastened before proceeding to the next section; use paper clips or small pieces of masking (not cellophane) tape to hold pieces while drying. Plastic spray fixative will keep your paper sculpture looking fresh and new for a long time to come.

INSTRUCTIONS

You need

- 1 pad tracing paper
- Paper Sculpture Patterns (pages 204-205)
- Enlarging Patterns materials (see page 206)
- Pen
- Soft lead (#1) pencil
- Pencil compass
- Triangle
- Steel straight edge
- Pushpin or large safety pin
- Artist's knife
- Cardboard cutting surface
- Scissors
- 9" x 9" or larger piece of corrugated cardboard
- Two 21" x 25" sheets white 2-ply smooth-finish paper
- 1 tube white glue
- Paper clips
- Masking tape
- One 8½" x 11" sheet typing paper
- Folded dish towel or other soft surface
- Sharp orange stick
- Five to seven 10"-long thin sticks or wires
- 28" length flower-wrapping wire on spool
- Newspaper
- 1 can plastic spray fixative

To prepare paper

Patterns

1. With tracing paper and Enlarging Patterns Materials, bring Paper Sculpture Pattern 1 up to full size. With pen and tracing paper, trace full-size Pats. 2-10. (Draw inner lines heavily on Pats. 7 and 8.)

2. Rub side of #1 pencil point on back of Pats. 1-6, 9 and 10 over lines to simulate carbon paper; then place Patterns face up on 2-ply paper and trace lines onto paper. Or place Pats. 1-6, 9 and 10 face up on 2-ply and with push-pin or safety pin, mark outline, inner lines and compass points of Patterns on 2-ply.

Cutting and Scoring

With artist's knife against straight edge on cardboard cutting surface, cut on straight cutting lines and score (half-cut) on scoring lines in Pats. 1-6, 9 and 10. If desired, cut curved edges with scissors. Practice scoring on scrap paper to reach desired pressure. Score circular lines slowly with knife; do not lift knife from paper.

To make centerpiece

Core

1. With scissors, cut an 8" circle from corrugated cardboard.

2. Cut a 10¼" x 5" rectangle from 2-ply. Cut 1" slashes across one 10¼" edge, about ⅜" apart. Roll into 3¾" diameter tube, overlapping edges 1". With white glue, glue overlapped edges together.

3. Draw a 3¾" circle in center of corrugated base. Spread heavy ring of glue around it (Fig. 1).

4. Place 2-ply tube upright on glue ring; let dry.

Grooved cone top (Pat. 2)

1. Carefully fold away from scored lines to obtain grooved-cone shape. Overlap straight edges and pull cone to a 5"-diameter base measurement; glue (Fig. 2).

2. Glue top rim (with slashed sections fanned slightly outward) to underside of Cone Top (Fig. 2).

Pleated Skirt (Pat. 1)

1. Fold along scored lines as pleats all around. Overlap 1" and glue 2 ends together.

2. Slip Pleated Skirt over Cone Top and Core. Place top of Skirt just under Cone lip (Fig. 3). Turn whole piece upside down and dab all points where pleated edge touches Cone Top with glue; let dry in this position.

Outer skirt and medallions (Pats. 3 and 4)

1. With sharp edge of scissors, curl lower curved flaps of 11-lobed Outer Skirt. Curl upper split strips tightly between fingers or around a pencil (Fig. 4). Form Skirt into ring and glue at overlap.

2. Slip Outer Skirt into place over Pleated Skirt and dab glue at most contact points around. With tape, hold piece in place; let dry (Fig. 5).

3. With each medallion (Pat. 4), form a grooved cone and glue overlap.

4. Glue medallions onto Outer Skirt beneath each top curl as in Fig. 6. With tape, hold piece in place; let dry.

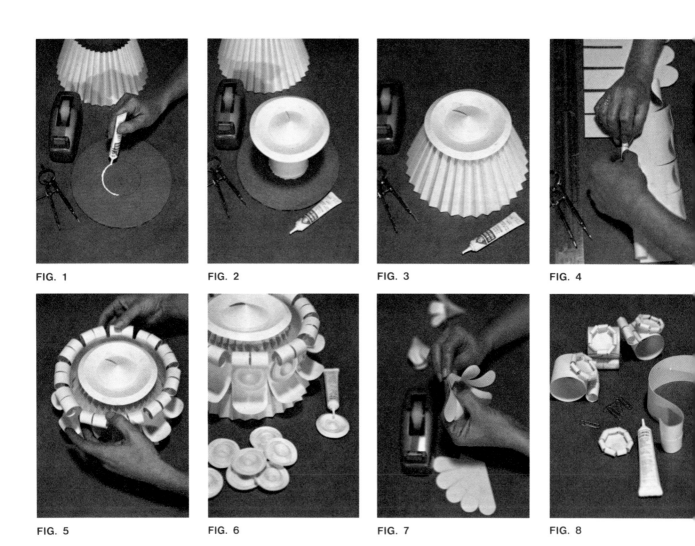

FIG. 1   FIG. 2   FIG. 3   FIG. 4

FIG. 5   FIG. 6   FIG. 7   FIG. 8

Flowers and stamen strips (Pat. 5)

1. Curl petals against sharp edge of scissors.

2. With artist's knife and straight edge, cut ten 7" x ¹⁄₁₆" stamen strips. Fold each in half to measure 3½" x ¹⁄₁₆". Curl ends slightly between finger and thumbnail. With dab of glue, attach folded end of Stamen near center point of Flower; repeat for all 10 Flowers.

3. Form Flower into Cone; overlap edges and glue (Fig. 7). Repeat for all Flowers.

Butterflies (Pats. 6, 7 and 8)

1. With pen and tracing-paper patterns, trace Pats. 7 and 8 outlines on typing paper; cut out. Place Pat. 7 outline over Pat. 7, place both on folded dish towel or other soft surface, and emboss by tracing gently over vein design with sharp orange stick or other rounded point. Repeat for Pat. 8. Repeat for as many Butterflies as desired.

2. Curl Butterfly bodies (Pat. 6) into tubes and glue at overlap. With glue, attach bodies to centers of butterfly wings.

3. With dabs of glue, secure one 10" stem in each of 5-7 Flowers and 1 wire support into each Butterfly body. Let dry. Twist 2 or more Butterfly wires together at lower end for sturdiness.

Assembling centerpiece

1. With knife, carefully make one ⅛" X-shaped slit in Cone Top for each Flower stem. With pushpin or large safety pin, make 1 pinhole in Cone Top for each Butterfly wire.

2. Insert Flower stems and Butterfly wires into Cone Top, arranging to various heights. Put a dab of glue at each hole to secure. Place a dab of glue on each remaining Flower and place Flowers directly on Cone Top. Let dry.

3. Place Centerpiece on newspaper to protect work surface. Spray entire piece with clear plastic fixative to protect from moisture and preserve curl.

To make napkin rings

1. Curl 1 end of Pat. 9 tightly around pencil. Form strips into 2" rings so curl is outside. Glue uncurled end to inside of ring and with tape or clips, hold piece in place. Let dry. (See Fig. 8.)

2. Curl spokes of Pat. 10 pieces toward center around pencil. Glue to napkin rings.

Macramé Swing and Holder

The craft of tying knots in cord to create designs has its origins blurred with the passing of time. Some experts think macramé began when the ancient Assyrians wore rope fringes on their robes. Others say it was 13th-century Arabs who created the craft; the word macramé itself comes from an Arabic word that means "embroidered veil." It is known that seagoing sailors have long tied extra rope into decorative pieces which they then sold, and in fact the knots used in macramé are the same ones sailors have always used.

Macramé today is used for wall hangings, jewelry, belts, purses, sculpture and many other items. Our swing and holder combine the beauty and practicality of this age-old craft. Make the swing in cotton seine twine and the holder in jute; both are strong fibers that will easily support a great deal of weight. The holder has a multitude of uses: for holding a fishbowl, a prized plant, the cookie jar. Hang the swing wherever there's some extra space— in a doorway, on a porch, from a tree. They're both perfect for kids and adults alike!

SWING SEAT INSTRUCTIONS

You need

- Yardstick
- Scissors
- Rubber bands
- Two 150' balls #48 (⅛" diameter) cotton seine twine
- Two 2" steel rings
- Cellophane tape
- White glue

To make

1. Cut ten 24' 6" cotton twine strands. Fold each strand in half to make twenty 12' 3" knotting strands. With lark's head knot (Fig. 1), tie each double strand at the half mark onto a 2" steel ring. With each strand, make butterfly (Fig. 2) 12" below ring. Wrap each strand with a rubber band to make strands easier to handle while working.

2. Beginning at center with strand 10 from left edge as a diagonal holding cord, tie 9 diagonal clove hitches (Fig. 3) to outer left edge to make diagonal bar. Repeat to right edge with strand 11 as diagonal holding cord to make diagonal bar to right.

3. Beginning at center again, tie alternating square knots (Fig. 4) tightly beneath diagonal bars to make a diamond-shaped area. Finish diamond-shaped area with diagonal bars using outer edge strands as holding cords— 1 from left, 1 from right. When the 2 diagonal bars meet in center, use the left holding cord as the knotting strand to tie last diagonal clove hitch around right holding cord.

4. Lay the outer left edge strand straight across all other strands so that it just touches the bottom of the diagonal bars above. Tape strand into that position. Tie 19 clove hitches (Fig. 5) around that strand to make horizontal bar.

5. Tie 11 rows of alternating square knots (Fig. 4).

6. Divide strands into 5 groups of 4 strands each. Tie a square knot braid (Fig. 6) of 32 square knots with each 4-strand group.

7. With all 20 strands, repeat alternating square knot pattern for 11 rows as in step 5. With outer left edge strand as holding cord, tie 19 clove hitches (Fig. 5), making a horizontal bar.

8. Repeat steps 2 and 3.

9. With lark's head variation (Fig. 7), attach second 2" steel ring. Begin with center 2 strands. Tie 1 lark's head variation (Fig. 7) to left side, 1 to right, 1 to left and so on around ring.

10. Turn swing seat over to work from back side. Tie one row half hitches (Fig. 8) to hold lark's head variation row in place. Trim all strands short and dab with glue.

FISH BOWL HANGER INSTRUCTIONS

You need

- One 4-oz. spool (75 yds.) colored 2-ply jute
- One 1½" steel ring
- One 7¾"-diameter embroidery hoop
- One 6"-diameter embroidery hoop
- Bowl, 9½" diameter, 6" high

To make

1. Cut sixteen 14' strands of jute. Thread all 16 strands through 1½" ring and slide ring halfway down strands. Divide 16 strands on 1 side into two 8-strand groups. With these 8 strands in each hand, tie a square knot (Fig. 9) around the 16 strands on other side of ring. Ring is now tied in center of 32 knotting strands. Hang ring on high hook or doorknob so you can work with both hands.

2. Place all 32 strands inside one 7¾" hoop. Bring hoop 8" below square knot and tie into position with 32 clove hitches (Fig. 5) spaced evenly around hoop. Work opposite sides at first to hold hoop level.

3. Two inches below hoop, tie a square knot (Fig. 9) with each 2 strands (16 square knots).

4. One inch below square knot row, tie a square knot with 1 strand from each of 2 knots above (16 square knots).

5. One inch below last row, tie 1 row of 8 alternating square knots (Fig. 4); use 1 strand from each of 2 knots above as holding cords and other strand from same 2 knots above as knotting strand.

6. Two inches below last row, tie 1 row of 8 alternating square knots.

7. One inch below last row, with same 2 holding cords and same 2 knotting strands from each square knot above, tie another row of square knots; this begins caterpillars (Fig. 10).

8. Repeat step 7 for 4 rows on each 2 holding cords, spacing rows 1" apart.

9. Slide the 5 rows of square knots upward on their holding cords making 8 caterpillars. Tie 1 tight square knot under each caterpillar.

10. Two inches below caterpillars, use 1 knotting strand from each 2 knots above as new holding cords. With 1 strand from each pair of holding cords above as new knotting strands, tie 12 granny knots (Fig. 11) to make a granny twist. Repeat to make 8 granny twists in all.

11. Three inches below granny twists, change holding cords. Tie 1 row alternating square knots (Fig. 4). Tie 2nd row of alternating square knots, 1½" below last row.

12. Eleven inches below last row, or leaving space needed to accommodate your bowl, attach 6" hoop with clove hitches (Fig. 5) spaced around hoop in 8 groups of 4.

13. In each group of 4 strands, with center 2 strands as holding cords and outer 2 strands as knotting strands, tie 8 square knots (Fig. 9).

14. Tie 7 rows alternating square knots (Fig. 4); they will automatically become close together as rows work toward center of hoop.

15. Divide the 32 strands into 3 groups (2 groups of 8 strands each, 1 group of 16 strands). With 16-strand group as holding cord and 2 groups of 8 strands as knotting strands, tie 7 granny knots (Fig. 11) to make granny twist.

16. Wrap 1 strand around all other strands; tie a half hitch (Fig. 8). With same strand, wrap around all strands and tie another half hitch.

17. Trim all strands even to about 8". Untwist each hanging strand to make tassel fringe. ○

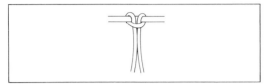

**FIG. 1
LARK'S HEAD KNOT**

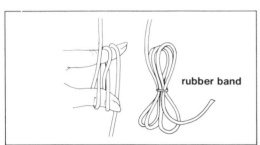

**FIG.2
BUTTERFLY**

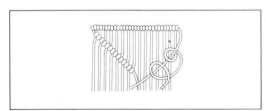

**FIG.3
DIAGONAL CLOVE HITCH**

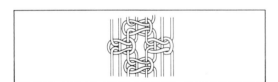

**FIG.4
ALTERNATING SQUARE KNOTS**

**FIG.5
CLOVE HITCH**

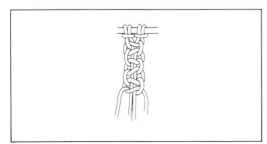

**FIG.6
SQUARE KNOT BRAID**

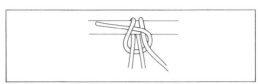

**FIG.7
LARK'S HEAD VARIATION**

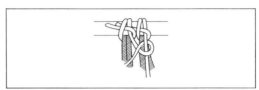

**FIG.8
HALF HITCH**

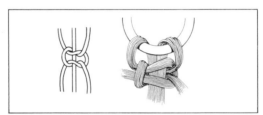

**FIG.9
SQUARE KNOT**

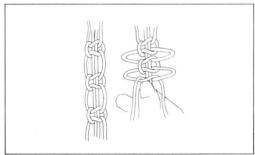

**FIG.10
CATERPILLAR**

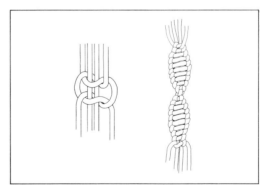

**FIG.11
GRANNY KNOT AND GRANNY TWIST**

Covered Desk Accessories

Paper or fabric and inexpensive purchased stationery supplies combine to make lovely coordinated desk accessories. Choose identical or contrasting coverings to brighten up desks at home or in the office, for students and professionals. Find all the materials you'll need at drugstores, variety stores, office- and art-supply stores and fabric shops. Wallpaper paste and careful cutting and folding make the job easy.

INSTRUCTIONS

You need
- Cardboard sheets
- Metal-edge ruler
- Heavy-duty mat knife
- Heavyweight mounting board
- 1 roll 2" surgical tape
- Orange stick (optional)
- 1 or 2 paper pads for each notebook
- Mulberry paper, decorator-weight wrapping paper or lightweight cotton fabrics
- Clear-drying, cold-water wallpaper paste
- 1" paintbrush
- Heavyweight cover stock
- Newspapers
- Contact cement
- Spring-type clothespins
- Cardboard tubing
- Pencils

To make 1- or 2-Pad Notebook

1. Line work table with cardboard to prevent marring surface. With metal-edge ruler and mat knife, cut front and back covers and spine from mounting board (Fig. 1A shows dimensions). If Covered Pencil will be adhered to spine, cut front and back ½" wider than pad.

2. Position covers and spine on work surface, wrong sides down, with 3/16" between covers and spine. Line up bottom edge with ruler to keep level. Cut piece of tape 1"-2" longer than spine. Center tape along spine so it extends to covers, sticky side down, and run finger along tape so spine and covers are joined. Do not press tape into crevices. Turn book so wrong side is up; fold tape over edge, creasing with thumbnail or orange stick (Fig. 1B). Cut a piece of tape ¼" shorter than spine. Press tape to spine only; run thumbnail along crevices so top tape makes contact with bottom tape. Press remaining tape to covers (Fig. 1B).

3. Cut paper or fabric ⅝" larger than book on all sides. Mark position of book on paper and cut across corners ¼"-⅜" from book corners. Mix small amount of wallpaper paste to a thick consistency according to package instructions. With paintbrush, coat wrong side of paper or fabric with paste; firmly press book onto paper, turn over and smooth out bubbles with edge of ruler or hand. Turn inside up, fold paper to inside and shape corners (Figs. 1C and 1D).

4. Cut strip of paper or fabric ¼" shorter and 2" wider than spine. Paste in place over spine, creasing along crevices (Fig. 1D). To make sleeve for pad, cut and fold cover stock as in Fig. 1E; paste in place. Repeat on other cover for 2-pad book. For 1-pad book, cut endpaper from cover stock slightly smaller than book cover and paste in place. If desired, paste paper pocket to bottom half of endpaper by folding under pocket edges and applying paste to side and bottom folded edges only.

5. Pressing book. Immediately insert flat book between 2 layers of newspaper, top with several heavy books and let dry overnight or until paste is completely dry. Scrape away any bits of stuck-on newspaper with mat knife. Insert cardboard backs of paper pads in sleeves.

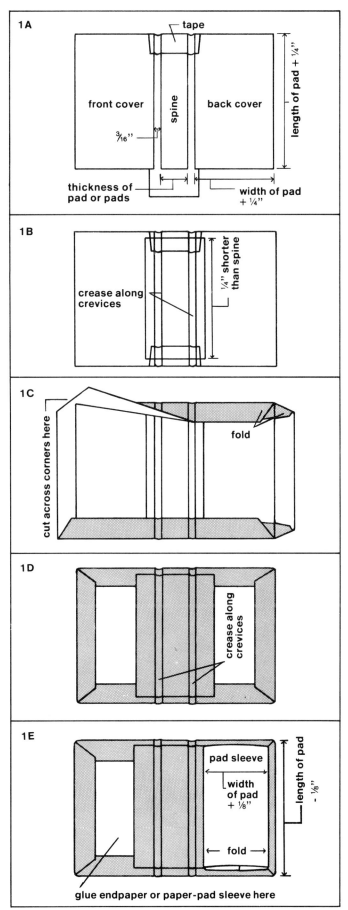

FIG. 1. NOTEBOOK
shading denotes right side of paper or fabric

To make Attached Pencil

Cut a 1"-wide strip of cover stock; with wallpaper paste, cover it with paper or fabric. Roll around pencil so ends overlap ⅜". Cut off excess. Remove pencil, paste overlap in place and let dry. Paste loop to spine, let dry, insert pencil.

To make Note Clip

With mat knife, cut 2 trapezoid- or circular-shaped pieces of mounting board for each clip (Fig. 2 or 3). Cover each piece with paper or fabric as in step 3 of Notebook Instructions and Figs. 2 or 3. With same paper or fabric, cover remaining side (Fig. 2). Press as in step 5 of Notebook Instructions. With contact cement, glue clothespin between 2 dry clip pieces.

To make Clipboard

Cut rectangle of desired size from mounting board. Cover 1 side with paper or fabric as in step 3 of Notebook Instructions. Cover remaining side and press as in step 5 of Notebook Instructions. Make circular clip as in Note Clip Instructions and Fig. 3, but use 1 circle only. Glue circular clip to top of rectangle with contact cement.

To make Pencil Box

1. Cut 4 rectangles of mounting board, each 3" x 4". With wallpaper paste, paste pieces into 4"-high box. Place box on mounting board, outline bottom with pencil, cut along lines and paste box to bottom.

2. Cut strip of paper or fabric 13" x 5½". Paste to sides of box, overlapping at 1 corner and allowing ½" excess at bottom. Fold ½" to bottom. Fold excess at top to inside of box, trimming at corners to eliminate bulk. Cover bottom with piece cut slightly smaller than bottom. Place a book or other weight on top of box and let dry overnight.

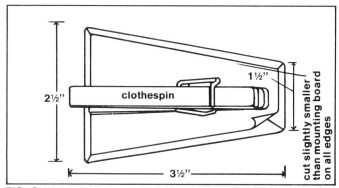

FIG. 2
TRAPEZOID NOTE CLIP

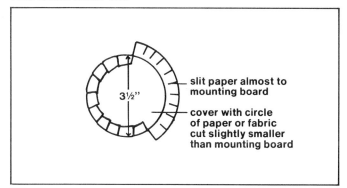

FIG. 3
CIRCULAR CLIP

To make Pencil Cup

Follow Pencil Box Instructions, using a 2" piece of cardboard tubing for sides and mounting board for bottom. Slit paper or fabric as in Fig. 3 before folding at top or bottom edges.

To make Covered Pencils

Cut a piece of paper or fabric 1½ times circumference of pencil x length of pencil from top to beginning of sharpened point. Apply wallpaper paste to wrong side of paper and roll up pencil in it. Wipe off excess paste. To sharpen, whittle with knife.

PATTERNS AND STITCHES

Soft Sculpture Patterns

Mother: 1 sq. = 4".
Baby: 1 sq. = 1".
Arrows indicate velveteen nap direction.
All seam allowances = ⅜" unless otherwise indicated.
Fold fabric right sides together to cut all "cut 2" pieces.

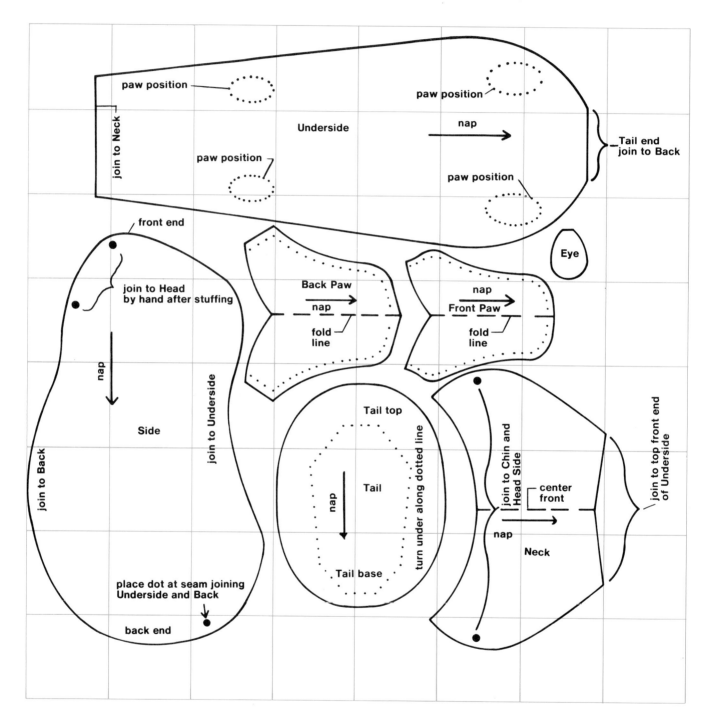

Mother

White velveteen	Gray velveteen	Black velveteen	White fur	Satin (lining)
Underside: Cut 1	Side: Cut 2	Eye: Cut 2	Tail: Cut 1	Ear: Cut 2
Back paw: Cut 2	Head side: Cut 2		Neck: Cut 1	
Front paw: Cut 2	Undertail: Cut 1			
Nose/Chin: Cut 1	Ear: Cut 2			
	Head top/back: Cut 1			
	Back: Cut 1			

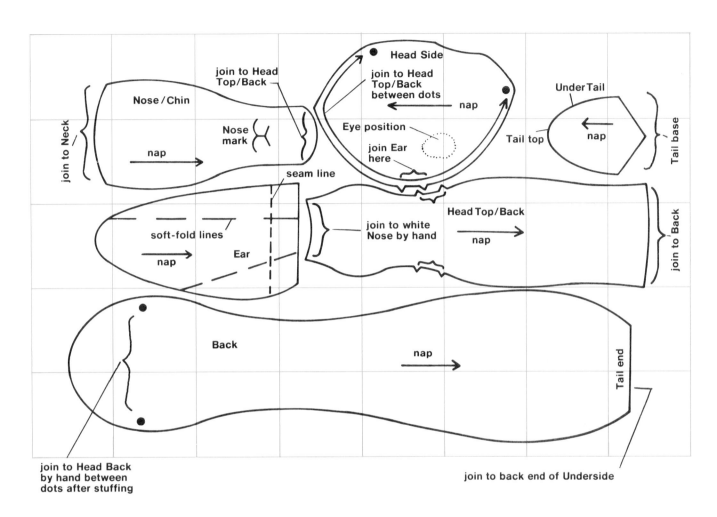

Nose/Chin

join to Neck

nap

Nose mark

join to Head Top/Back

seam line

Head Side

join to Head Top/Back between dots

nap

Eye position

join Ear here

Under Tail

Tail top

nap

Tail base

soft-fold lines

nap

Ear

join to white Nose by hand

Head Top/Back

nap

join to Back

Back

nap

Tail end

join to Head Back by hand between dots after stuffing

join to back end of Underside

Babies

White velveteen

Underside: Cut 3
Back paw: Cut 6
Front paw: Cut 6
Side: Cut 4
Nose/Chin: Cut 3
Head side: Cut 2
Ear: Cut 2
Head top/back: Cut 4
Back: Cut 2

Gray velveteen

Side: Cut 2
Head side: Cut 4
Undertail: Cut 3
Ear: Cut 4
Head to/back: Cut 2
Back: Cut 1

Black velveteen:
Eye: Cut 6

White fur

Tail: Cut 3
Neck: Cut 3

Satin (lining)

Ear: Cut 6

Rug Patterns

Rug Pattern 1
Motif of Squares

Rug Pattern 2
Color Pattern

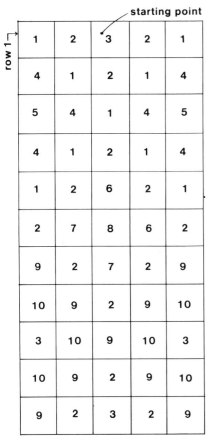

starting point

row 1

1	2	3	2	1
4	1	2	1	4
5	4	1	4	5
4	1	2	1	4
1	2	6	2	1
2	7	8	6	2
9	2	7	2	9
10	9	2	9	10
3	10	9	10	3
10	9	2	9	10
9	2	3	2	9

Rug Pattern 3
Corner and border design

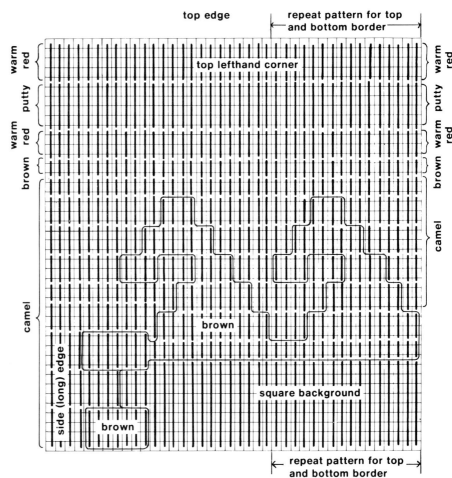

top edge

repeat pattern for top and bottom border

warm red

putty

warm red

brown

camel

warm red

putty

warm red

brown

camel

top lefthand corner

side (long) edge

brown

brown

square background

repeat pattern for top and bottom border

Square 1	Square 2	Square 3	Square 4	Square 5
A = warm red	A = putty	A = putty	A = putty	A = salmon
B = cream	B = salmon	B = cream	B = cream	B = cream
C = brown	C = brown	C = brown	C = brown	C = brown
D = brown	D = brown	D = putty	D = brown	D = salmon
E = brown	E = brown	E = putty	E = warm red	E = putty
F = brown	F = brown	F = brown	F = brown	F = brown
G = camel	G = sienna	G = salmon	G = salmon	G = putty
H = warm red	H = cream	H = sienna	H = blue	H = sienna

Square 6	Square 7	Square 8	Square 9	Square 10
A = putty	A = putty	A = blue	A = sienna	A = putty
B = cream	B = cream	B = cream	B = salmon	B = cream
C = brown	C = brown	C = blue	C = warm red	C = brown
D = putty	D = brown	D = brown	D = brown	D = brown
E = putty	E = brown	E = warm red	E = brown	E = warm red
F = brown	F = brown	F = brown	F = brown	F = brown
G = salmon	G = warm red	G = warm red	G = camel	G = warm red
H = sienna	H = sienna	H = camel	H = warm red	H = blue

Papered Screen Pattern

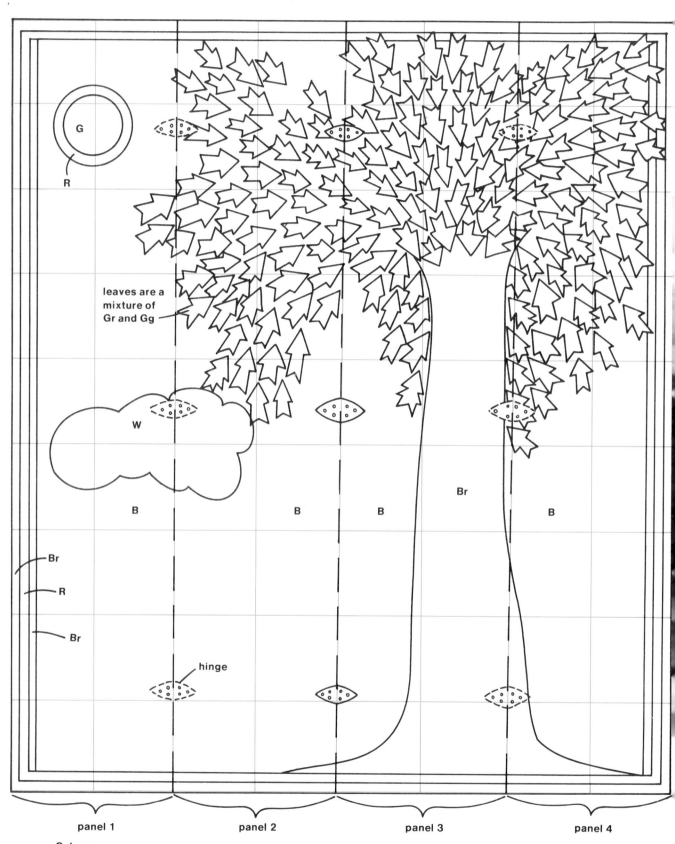

leaves are a
mixture of
Gr and Gg

hinge

panel 1 panel 2 panel 3 panel 4

Colors

B = blue   Gg = gold
Br = brown   R = red
Gr = green   G = gold   1 sq. = 8"

Seminole Apron Pattern

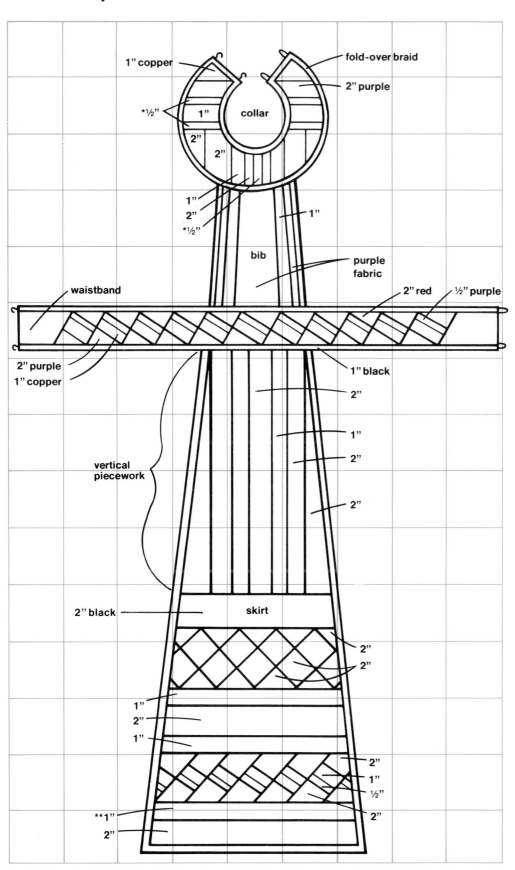

1" copper

fold-over braid

2" purple

*½" 1" collar

2"

2"

1"
2"
*½"

bib

1"

waistband

purple
fabric

2" red ½" purple

2" purple
1" copper

1" black

2"

1"

2"

vertical
piecework

2"

2" black skirt

2"
2"

1"
2"
1"

2"
1"
½"

**1"
2"

2"

*fold 1" width in half
**fold 2" width in half

1 sq. = 4"

Ornament Patterns

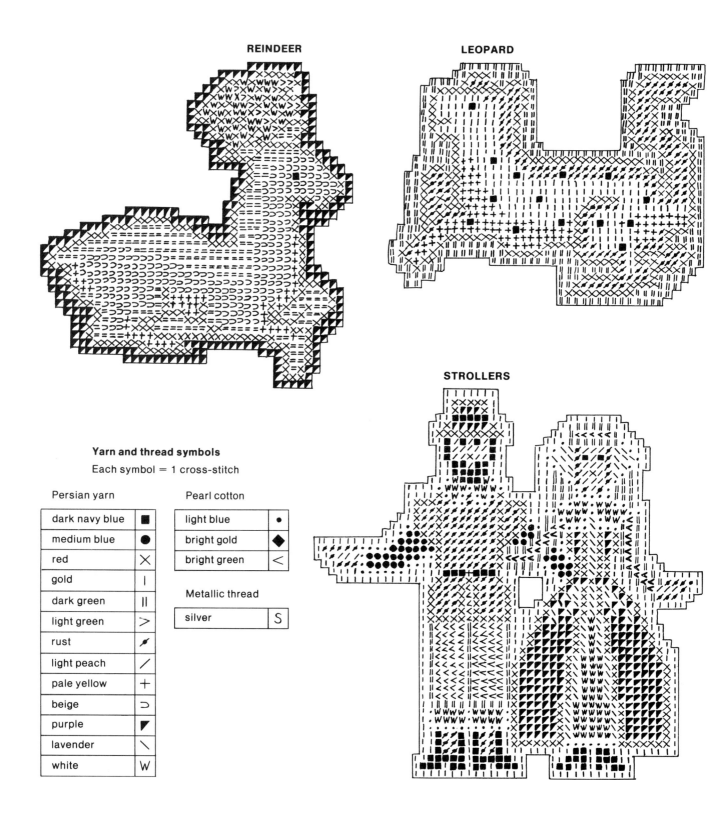

REINDEER

LEOPARD

STROLLERS

Yarn and thread symbols

Each symbol = 1 cross-stitch

Persian yarn	
dark navy blue	◼
medium blue	●
red	✕
gold	│
dark green	‖
light green	>
rust	⟋
light peach	╱
pale yellow	+
beige	⊃
purple	◤
lavender	╲
white	W

Pearl cotton	
light blue	•
bright gold	◆
bright green	<

Metallic thread	
silver	S

HORSEMAN

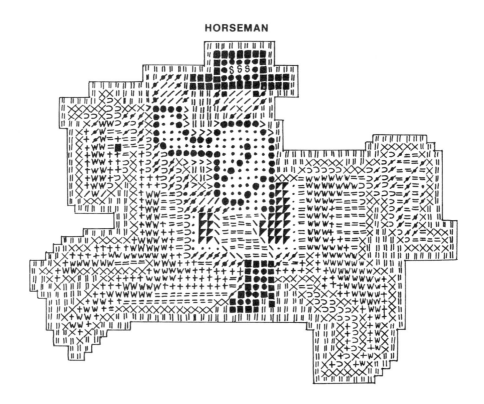

MUSICIAN

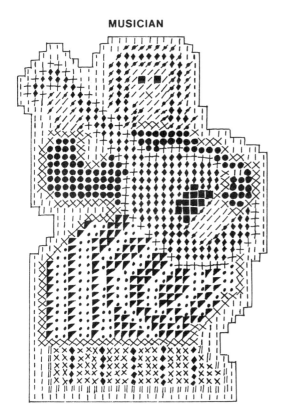

ANGEL

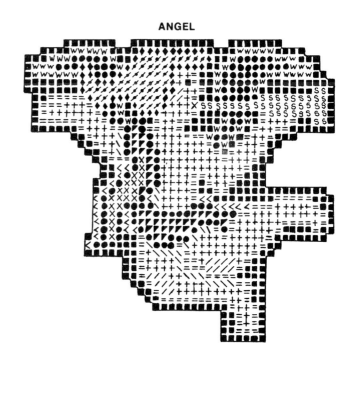

Wood Sculpture Pattern

1 sq. = 1"

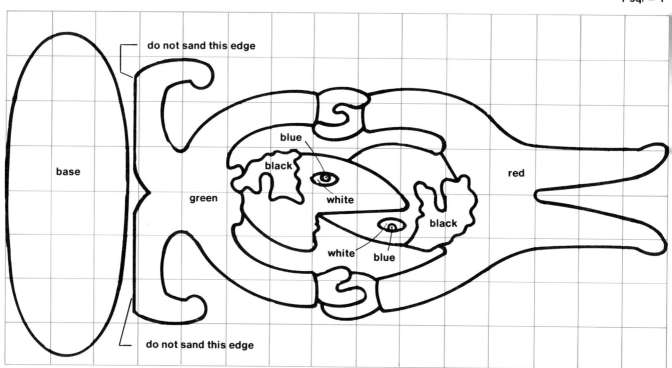

Block Printing Patterns

Embroidered Apron Patterns

Embroidered Apron Pattern 1

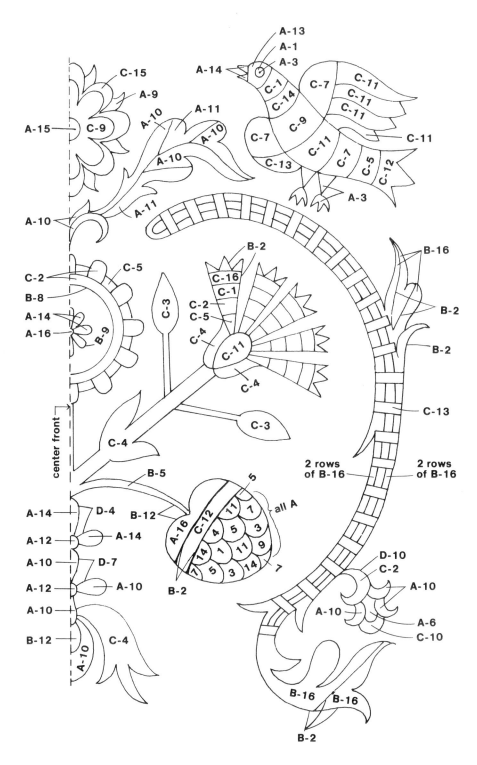

Stitches

A = satin stitch
B = chain stitch
C = Cretan feather stitch
D = stem stitch

Colors

1 = white
2 = gold
3 = rose
4 = red
5 = dark green
6 = medium green
7 = violet
8 = bright gold
9 = yellow
10 = bright blue
11 = dark blue
12 = gold-brown
13 = dark brown
14 = beige
15 = medium brown
16 = black

Embroidered Apron Pattern 2

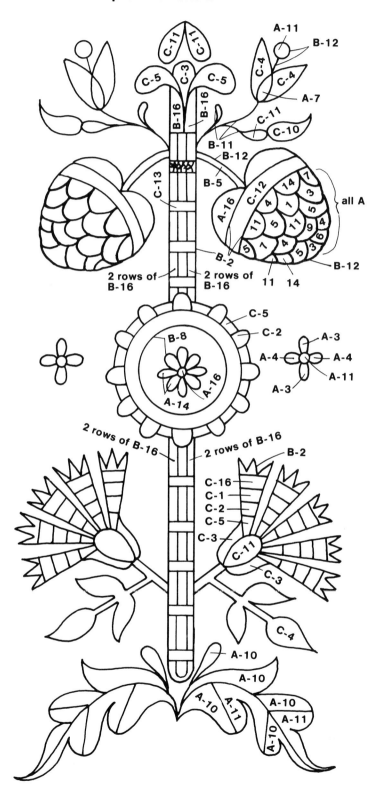

Embroidered Apron Pattern 3

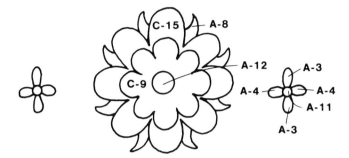

Embroidered Apron Pattern 4

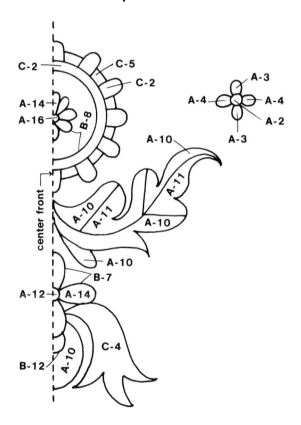

Embroidered Apron Pattern 5

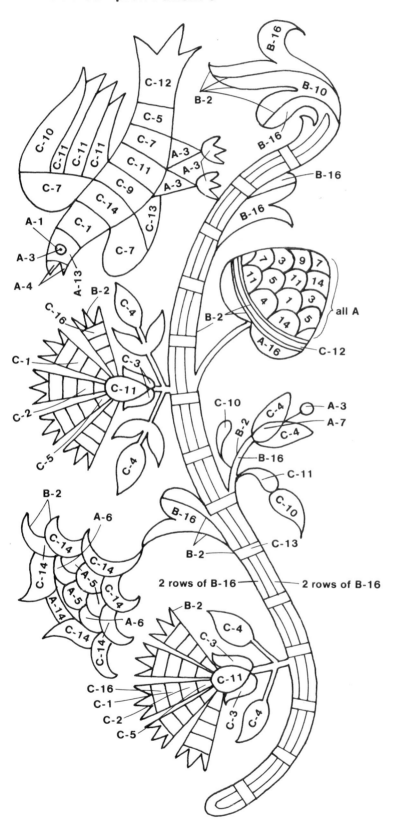

Sleeping Bag Patterns

Sleeping Bag Pattern 1

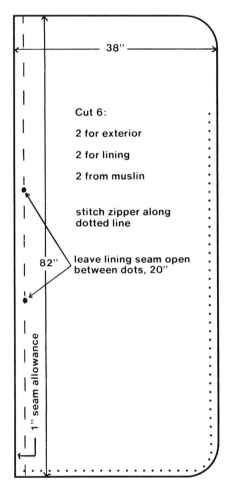

38"

Cut 6:

2 for exterior

2 for lining

2 from muslin

stitch zipper along
dotted line

leave lining seam open
between dots, 20"

82"

1" seam allowance

Sleeping Bag Pattern 2

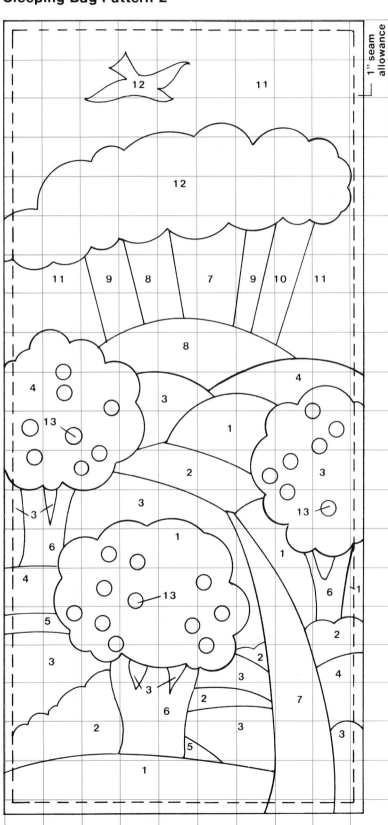

1" seam allowance

1 sq. = 4"

Suggested colors

1 = bright green
2 = brown-green
3 = medium green
4 = kelly green
5 = dark green
6 = brown
7 = gold
8 = yellow
9 = orange
10 = peach
11 = blue
12 = white
13 = pink

General Acrylic Instructions

Instructions for making acrylic desk accessories begin on page 68. Before you begin working with acrylic plastic, become familiar with these basic techniques.

SCRIBE-AND-BREAK CUTTING

This method can be used for straight lines only. Work on a flat surface that can take rough treatment or place several layers of cardboard under your work; as the knife blade comes off the acrylic it will sink into the surface below. Do not remove protective paper from acrylic. Each scribing must run the full length or width of the acrylic piece being cut for a successful break.

You need

- Metal or metal-edged ruler longer than the longest measurement you will be cutting
- Pencil
- Acrylic sheet
- Knife for cutting acrylic
- ¾'' dowel rod same length as ruler or table edge

To cut

1. With ruler and pencil, draw cutting lines on protective paper. Line up edge of ruler with pencil line and pull knife along the line 10-20 times to form a scribed line (groove) (Fig. 1A). Knife should make a scraping sound; be sure knife always cuts to edge of acrylic.

2. Place dowel rod on firm, flat surface and position acrylic with groove running along center of rod. Apply downward pressure to both sides of groove (Fig. 1B). Acrylic will break at groove. Use table edge in place of dowel rod if desired. Place groove exactly along the edge of a work table or counter with smaller portion of acrylic hanging over edge. With hand firmly on acrylic, apply pressure with palm of hand in sharp downward motion on overhanging piece, while tightly holding acrylic to table with other hand. If break is ragged or not perpendicular to acrylic surface, follow Sanding Instructions (below) to smooth and straighten edge.

3. For a long break, begin pressure at one edge and work along groove to other edge.

ELECTRIC-SAW CUTTING

Acrylic can be cut with a table (circular) saw, band saw, saber saw, jig saw or circular hand saw. Consult manufacturer's instructions on working with acrylic.

CUTTING CURVES

You need

- Grease pencil
- C-clamp
- Coping saw, saber saw or band saw
- Acrylic sheet

To cut

Mark the curve with grease pencil, clamp acrylic to work table and saw along mark (Fig. 2). For saber saw or band saw, consult manufacturer's instructions. Sand curved edges without using sanding block (see Sanding Instructions below).

DRILLING

You need

- C-clamp
- Acrylic sheet
- Scraps of acrylic or piece of plywood
- ³⁄₁₆'' drill bit for acrylic
- Manual or electric hand drill

To drill

Do not remove protective paper from acrylic. Clamp acrylic to work table with C-clamp, backing up the drilling area with scrap of acrylic or plywood (Fig. 2) to prevent chipping. Fit drill bit to drill and drill holes in appropriate positions.

1A

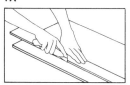

1B

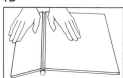

FIG.1
SCRIBE-AND-BREAK CUTTING

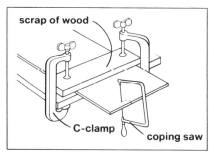

FIG. 2

SANDING AND POLISHING

All cut edges of acrylic must be sanded. Polish only those that will not be bonded.

You need

- #150 wet and dry sandpaper
- Sanding block
- #600 wet and dry sandpaper
- Acrylic polish
- Small dish of water
- Cut acrylic sheet

To sand and polish

1. Sand edges that will be bonded with #150 sandpaper until edge is completely free of irregularities or saw marks. Sanding block must always be at 90° angle to sheet surface. Sand with #600 sandpaper until edge is very smooth.

2. To polish, sand edges that are to be finished (not bonded) according to acrylic-polish manufacturer's instructions. Do not polish edges that will be bonded.

BONDING (Cementing)

Bonding acrylic to acrylic is done with a solvent that dissolves the surfaces. These surfaces then harden as they set, fusing the pieces together. Always use solvent in well-ventilated area. If solvent should trickle between acrylic and work surface, an impression of the work surface will be left in the softened acrylic. The impression can usually be removed by sanding and polishing (see above). Bond only when room and solvent temperatures are above 65°F.

You need

- Porcelain enamel or Formica work surface, or scrap piece of smooth Masonite paneling or sheet of glass as work surface
- #150 sandpaper
- Acrylic solvent
- Applicator

To bond

Remove ½" border or all of protective paper from acrylic. Fill applicator with solvent. With masking tape to hold pieces together (when necessary), place acrylic pieces together in desired position. Apply solvent to acrylic at 1 point along joining, using gentle, even pressure. Apply at corner when 3 pieces come together (Fig. 3A); apply near 1 end of seam when 2 pieces come together (Fig. 3B). Solvent will flow along area common to both surfaces. If solvent should spill on protective paper or elsewhere on acrylic, do not wipe it away. It will evaporate.

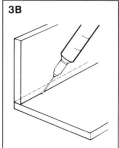

FIG.3
BONDING

Backpack Pattern

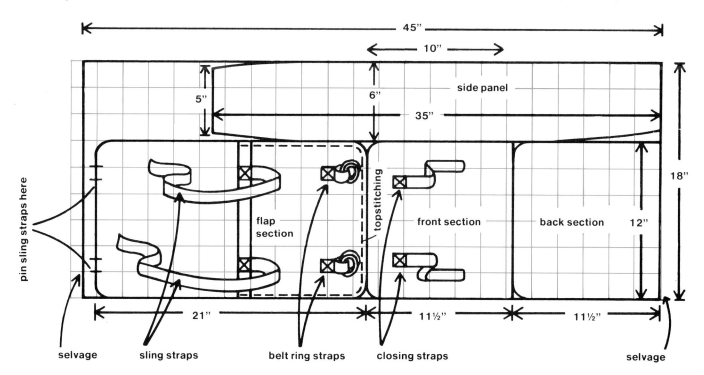

1 sq. = 2"   stitch straps to backpack with X-in-square

Wedding Dress Patterns

Stitches

A = straight stitch
B = satin stitch
C = buttonhole stitch
D = stem stitch
E = chain stitch
F = French knot
G = long and short stitch
H = couching stitch

Colors

1 = white pearl cotton
2 = ecru pearl cotton
3 = white Persian yarn
4 = very pale yellow Persian yarn
5 = beige Persian yarn
6 = light brown Persian yarn
7 = rosy beige Persian yarn
8 = rust Persian yarn

Wedding Dress Pattern 1

1 sq. = 1 in.

Wedding Dress Pattern 2

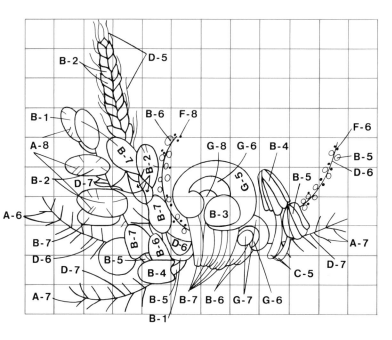

Embroidered Shirt Patterns

Embroidered Shirt Pattern 1

POCKET

Embroidered Shirt Pattern 2

FRONT TAB

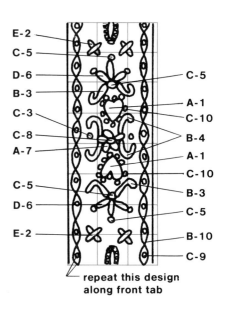

repeat this design
along front tab

Embroidered Shirt Pattern 3

CUFF

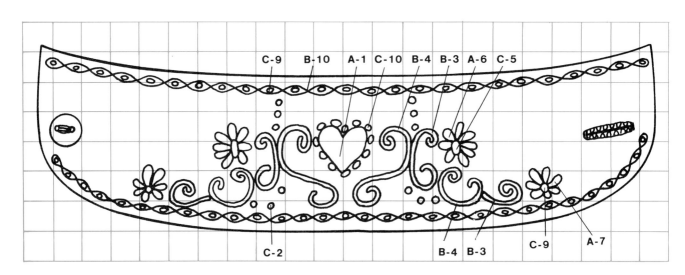

Embroidered Shirt Pattern 4

COLLAR

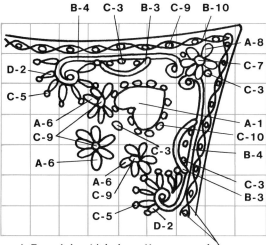

work French knot/chain pattern around
entire edge of collar

Colors

1 = pink
2 = blue
3 = light green
4 = dark green
5 = orange
6 = lavender
7 = gold
8 = red
9 = yellow
10 = white

Stitches

A = satin stitch
B = chain stitch
C = French knot
D = lazy daisy
E = cross-stitch

Silkscreen Pattern

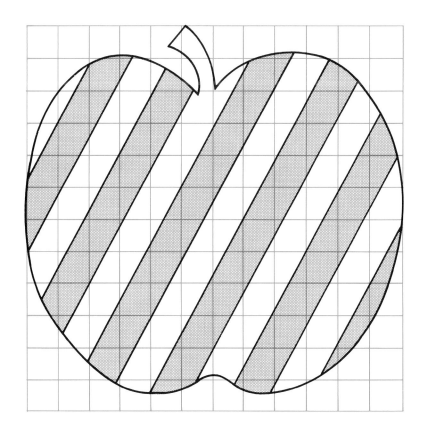

key

red   green

1 sq. = ⅜"

Tray Pattern

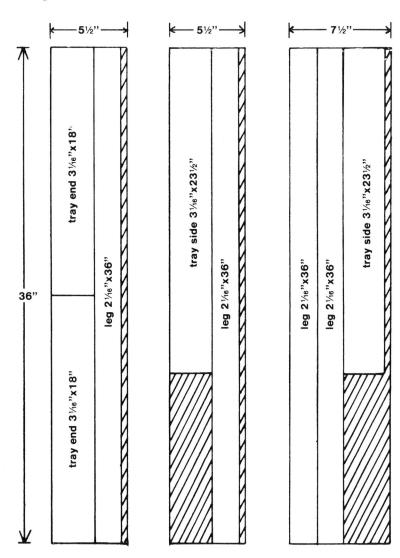

Tile Pattern

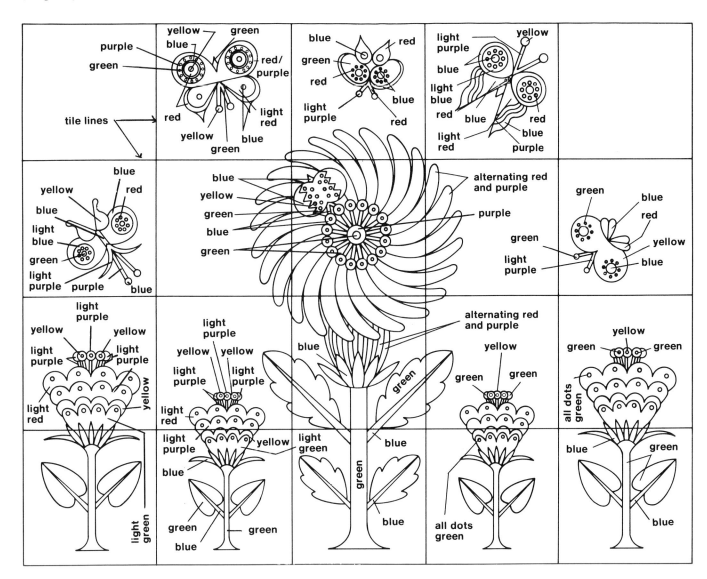

Tie-dye Pattern

Butterfly design

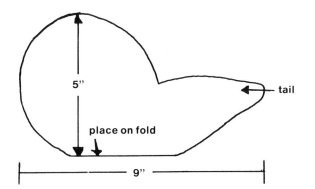

Quickpoint Patterns

TULIP BRICK   RIBBON BRICK

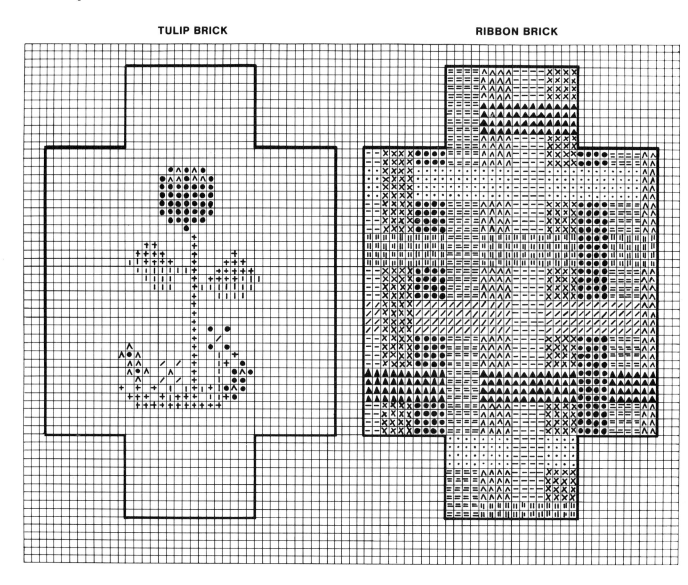

Colors

yellow	☐
orange	●
light orange	╱
dark green	✚
light green	❙
pink	∧
bright green	❚❚
chartreuse	✘
purple	━
lavender	═
red	•
turquoise	▲

Embroidered Sweater Patterns

Embroidered Sweater Pattern 1

Colors

1 = light blue
2 = rose
3 = red
4 = light green
5 = gold

Stitches

A = satin stitch
B = stem stitch
C = lazy daisy

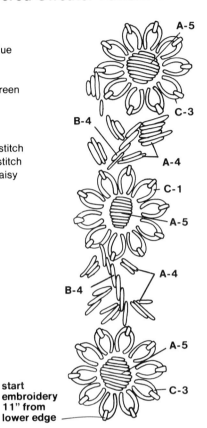

start embroidery 11" from lower edge

Embroidered Sweater Pattern 2

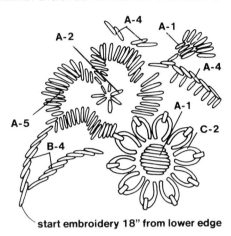

start embroidery 18" from lower edge

Machine Embroidery Patterns

squares should butt up against each other without overlapping

FIG. 1

Mola Patterns

Mola Pattern 1

1 sq. = 1"

fold —

Mola Pattern 2

1 sq. = 1"

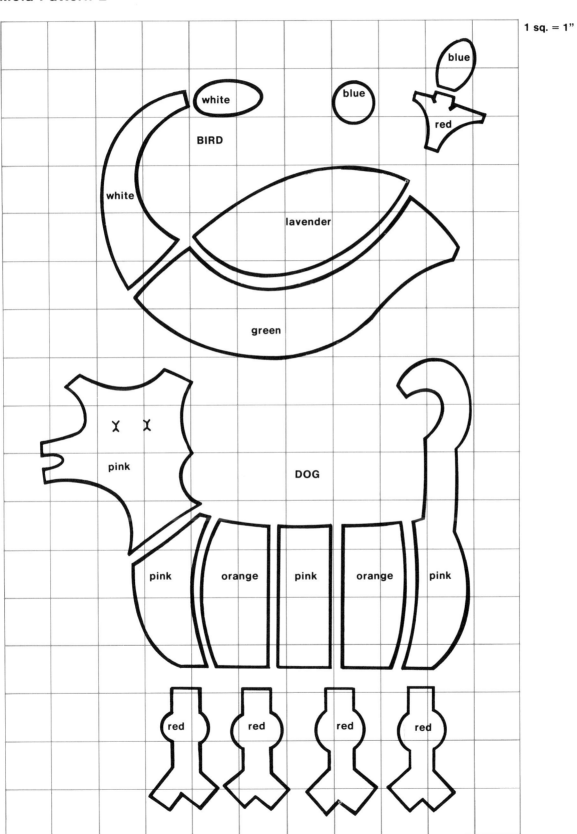

Plant Patterns

Plant Pattern 1

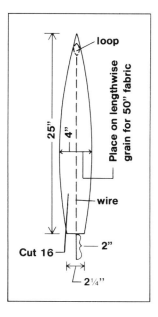

loop

Place on lengthwise grain for 50" fabric

25"

4"

wire

Cut 16 — 2"

2¼"

Plant Pattern 2

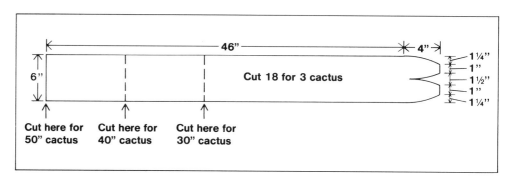

46"

4"

6"

1¼"
1"
1½"
1"
1¼"

Cut 18 for 3 cactus

Cut here for 50" cactus

Cut here for 40" cactus

Cut here for 30" cactus

Paper Sculpture Patterns

Paper Sculpture Pattern 1
pleated skirt—cut 1

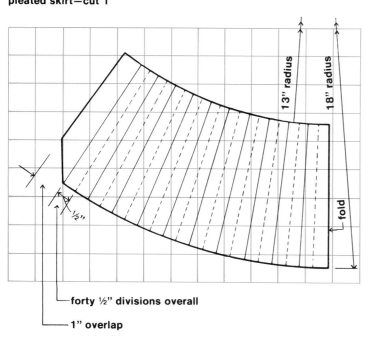

13" radius

18" radius

fold

½"

forty ½" divisions overall

1" overlap

Pattern code

Cutting lines	———
Scoring lines for topsides	———
Scoring lines for undersides	- - - - -
Overlaps	— — —
Compass points	+
Positioning points	⊕
Slits	x

1 sq. = 1"

Paper Sculpture Pattern 2
grooved cone top—cut 1

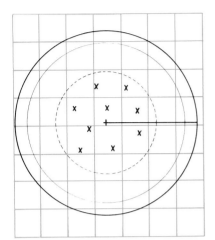

Paper Sculpture Pattern 3
outer skirt—cut 11

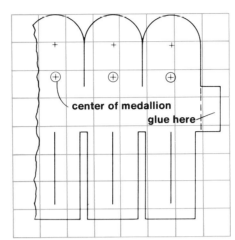

center of medallion

glue here

Paper Sculpture Pattern 4
outer skirt medallion—cut 11

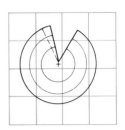

Paper Sculpture Pattern 5
flowers—cut 10

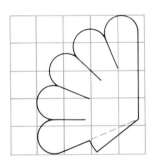

Paper Sculpture Pattern 6
butterfly bodies—cut 1 or more

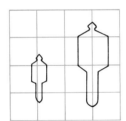

Paper Sculpture Pattern 7
large butterfly—cut 1 or more

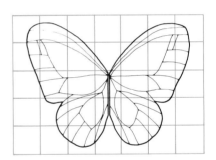

Paper Sculpture Pattern 8
small butterfly—cut 1 or more

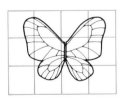

Paper Sculpture Pattern 9
napkin ring—cut 4

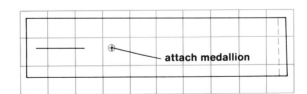

attach medallion

Paper Sculpture Pattern 10
napkin ring medallion—cut 4

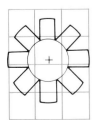

Enlarging Patterns

Whenever possible, the patterns in this section are shown full size. Patterns that are too large to be shown full size are drawn on a grid to simplify the enlarging procedure. Each of the grids is drawn to a scale that is indicated with the pattern; for example, 1 sq. = 1"; 1 sq. = 2".

Instructions

You need

- 1 or more large sheets of brown wrapping paper or paper specified in project instructions
- Ruler
- Pen
- Pencil
- Scissors

To make

1. With ruler, pen and paper, draw a grid of squares the full size indicated on the pattern; for example, when the pattern says 1 sq. = 1", draw a grid of 1" squares on the paper.

2. With pencil, copy the pattern onto the drawn grid square by square as it appears on the printed grid. Be sure to keep the part of the design in each square in its correct proportion as you copy it. Go over finished full-size pattern lines with pen.

3. With scissors, cut out the full-size pattern you have drawn and proceed as the instructions indicate.

Transferring Patterns

After you have enlarged a pattern, or when the pattern is drawn in this book to full size, the instructions might tell you to transfer it to the material with which you are working. Use dressmaker's carbon paper, available at notions counters, to transfer the patterns. To trace use a dressmaker's tracing wheel or a pointed orange stick.

Do not lean heavily on the carbon paper as you trace or ink smudges will appear on the fabric. Before you begin, practice on a scrap of the fabric to determine the amount of pressure you need to obtain a clear line. Use light-colored carbon for dark fabrics, dark carbon for light fabrics.

Instructions

You need

- Artist's tracing paper (optional)
- Fine-line felt-tip pen (optional)
- Dressmaker's carbon paper
- Dressmaker's tracing wheel or pointed orange stick
- Pins or tape
- Fabric

To make

1. If desired, place a sheet of artist's tracing paper over the pattern. With fine-line felt-tip pen, trace the pattern onto the paper.

2. Position pattern face up (or face down for a reverse image) on the fabric. Pin or tape in place, leaving an opening for carbon.

Stuffing Pillows and Other Pieces

When you need to select fabric for pillow backs, choose one of a similar weight to pillow front in a matching or contrasting color.

Instructions

You need

- Additional fabric for backing (optional)
- Pillow fabric
- Ruler
- Tailor's chalk
- Stuffing as specified in pillow instructions
- Knitting needle

To make

1. Cut the backing to the same size as the front.

2. With ruler and tailor's chalk, mark seam lines to allow ⅝" seam.

3. Pin back to front with right sides together. Stitch along seam lines leaving a 3" opening (longer for larger pieces). Press, trim seam allowances to ½" and turn right side out through opening.

4. Insert stuffing through opening until the piece is filled to desired firmness; as pillow is used stuffing will pack down slightly. With knitting needle or other pointed object work stuffing into corners.

5. When stuffing is complete, hand stitch opening closed.

Knitting

General Information

Knitting is a centuries-old craft whose usefulness and practicality—and beauty—have always made it popular. With just a pair of pointed needles, some yarn and a few basic stitches you can use knitting to make a wide variety of garments as well as decorative wall hangings and other pieces.

Be sure to keep your needles in the correct position (as shown in the figures) for the stitch on which you are working. Practice keeping your stitches even so the finished piece will have a look of uniformity. Even stitches are particularly important when you are knitting a garment, since without them the garment will not fit correctly.

Read the instructions all the way through before you begin a project. While working, though, don't read ahead; finish each part of each step before going on to the next. It might be helpful to draw a line through the instructions with a pencil as you complete them.

Stitches and terms

Knitting instructions are written using many abbreviations. The abbreviations are shown in parentheses after the stitch or term.

Casting on (co) (Fig. 1)

Knitting instructions will tell you to cast on a certain number of stitches to begin a project. Leave a yarn tail that many inches long and make a slip knot in the yarn over 1 needle. Wrap the yarn around your left hand (arrow shows position of tail) and insert needle under tail, then from right to left under yarn wrapped around index finger (Fig. 1A). Pull this loop through 1st loop, letting yarn come off thumb (Fig. 1B). A 2nd loop is on hook; 1 stitch is cast on.

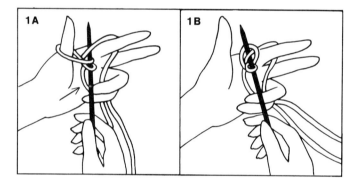

Knit (k) (Fig. 2)

Hold needle with cast-on stitches in left hand so that end of yarn (not tail) is to right and rear of needle. Insert other needle left to right through back of 1st stitch on left needle. Bring yarn counterclockwise around right needle (Fig. 2A) so that yarn end passes between needles and forms loop. Bring end of right needle over loop and through stitch, from right to left under left needle; a new loop is formed on right needle (Fig. 2B). Slip old stitch off left needle; 1 knit stitch is made (Fig. 2C). Continue working in this manner, keeping yarn end in back of needles. When row is completed, turn right needle and place in left hand. Continue as above.

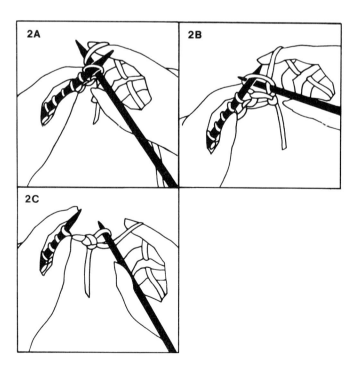

Purl (p) (Fig. 3)

Purl is the reverse of knit. Hold needle with cast-on stitches in left hand so that end of yarn (not tail) is to right and front of needle. Insert other needle left to right through front of 1st stitch on left needle. Bring yarn end around right needle counterclockwise to form loop (Fig. 3A). Bring end of needle over loop and through stitch from left to right (Fig. 3B). Slip old stitch over left needle; 1 purl stitch is made (Fig. 3C). Continue working in this manner, keeping yarn end in front of needles. When row is completed, turn right needle and place in left hand. Continue as above.

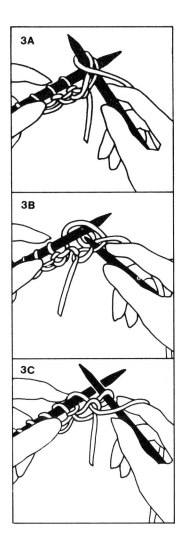

Binding off (Fig. 4)

Binding off is used to prevent edges from raveling. Always bind off in pattern stitch unless otherwise specified. Bind off ribbing in established ribbing pattern. Knit (purl) 1st 2 stitches of row. Using point of left needle, slip 1st new stitch over 2nd new stitch and off right needle (Fig. 4A). Knit (purl) 3rd stitch; slip 2nd stitch over 3rd and off right needle. Repeat procedure to end of row (Fig. 4B).

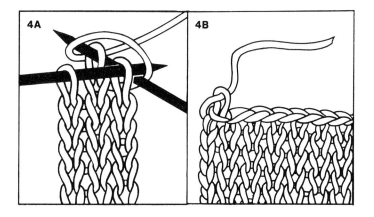

Increase (inc) (Fig. 5)

To increase in knit row: Knit one stitch on 1st stitch of row. Do not slip old stitch off left needle. Knit again into same stitch (Fig. 5A) but this time in back of stitch, from right to left (Fig. 5B). There will now be 2 stitches on right needle. Slip stitch off left needle. To increase in purl row: Purl one stitch on 1st stitch of row. Do not slip old stitch off left needle. Purl again into same stitch but this time in back of stitch. There will now be 2 stitches on right needle. Slip stitch off left needle.

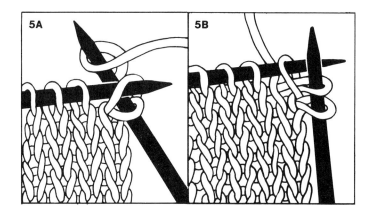

Decrease (dec) (Fig. 6)

To decrease at end of row or after raglan sleeve (shoulder): Knit (purl) 2 stitches together (Fig. 6A shows decrease slanting to right; Fig. 6B shows decrease slanting to left). To decrease at beginning of row or before raglan sleeve (shoulder) (Fig. 6C): Slip 1st stitch from left to right needle. Knit (purl) 2nd stitch. Pass slipped stitch over worked stitch and off right needle.

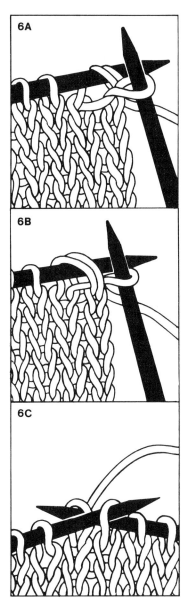

Yarn over (yo) (Fig. 7)

This method also increases stitches. In knit row (Fig. 7A) bring yarn end from back to front of right needle. A loop will be formed. Knit next stitch as usual. In purl row (Fig. 7B), wrap yarn counter-clockwise once around right needle. A loop will be formed. Purl next stitch as usual.

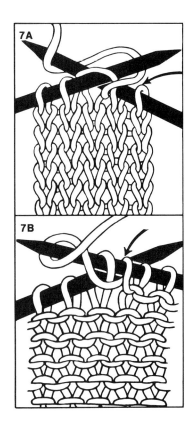

Slip stitch (sl st) (Fig. 8)

Keeping yarn in back of work, insert needle in stitch as if to purl (Fig. 8A). Slide the stitch from left to right needle. This is the most common way of slipping a stitch. Instructions might specify slipping a stitch by inserting needle as if to knit (Fig. 8B). Do so, then slide the stitch from left to right needle.

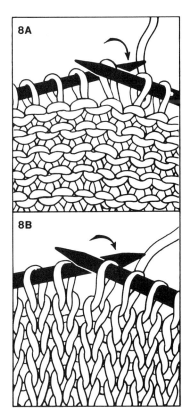

Garter stitch

Knit all rows. Both sides of knitting will appear the same.

Moss stitch

Work a knit stitch over a purl stitch and a purl stitch over a knit stitch. This stitch is used in cable.

Pick up and knit

Always work from right side, unless otherwise directed. Working from left to right on neckline (starting from right shoulder, working across back neck edge, down left-front neck edge): With right side facing and neckline at top, insert left needle through work. Wrap yarn around needle and pull back through work. A loop (stitch) is formed. Knit this stitch. Repeat number of times specified. (Stitches on holder are knitted directly from holder). Working from right to left on neckline (starting from right shoulder, working across right neck edge, across front neck edge): With right side facing and neckline at top, insert right needle through work. Wrap yarn around needle and pull back through work. A loop (stitch) is formed. Repeat number of times specified; then knit one row. Picking up along armholes may be done either left to right or right to left.

Popcorn stitch

Knit into front of stitch, knit into back of same stitch, knit into front, knit into back, knit into front, pull 4th, 3rd, 2nd and 1st stitches over 5th stitch.

Reverse stockinette stitch

Knit one row, purl one row, repeat. Purl is right side of work.

Ribbing (rib)

On even number of stitches, knit 1 stitch, purl 1 stitch every row. On odd number of stitches, purl 1 stitch, knit 1 stitch on odd rows and knit 1 stitch, purl 1 stitch on even rows.

Seed stitch

Knit 1, purl 1 across row. Knit all purls and purl all knits on next row.

Stockinette stitch (st st)

Knit one row, purl one row, repeat. Knit is right side of work.

Gauge

Be sure you knit to the gauge specified in the instructions. To test your gauge, cast on 20 to 30 stitches using needle size given in the instructions. Work 3" in stitch used for greatest proportion of garment. Smooth out swatch, pin down and measure. If you have more stitches and rows to the inch than specified, use larger needles. If you have fewer, use smaller needles. Knit new swatches with different-sized needles until the gauge is correct.

Markers

(a) To mark a row on straight needles (as for underarms), tie small piece of contrasting yarn in first and last stitch of row. (b) To mark a stitch in a row, use commercial plastic markers or loops of contrasting yarn. Place 1 marker or yarn loop on needle before and after stitch. Slip markers to right needle before and after stitch is worked. (c) To mark end of row on circular needle, place purchased plastic marker or yarn loop on needle after last stitch of row when casting on and before joining to first stitch. Always slip marker from left point to right point when it comes around. (d) To mark divisions in rows on circular needles, place marker on right needle after proper number of stitches have been worked (e.g., work 54 stitches, mark beginning of left raglan, work 20 stitches, mark end of left raglan).

Stitch holders

Stitches are usually worked directly from holder. (a) To hold stitches that are not currently being worked, as in necklines that are not bound off, use a safety pin-shaped stitch holder. Slip specified stitches onto holder and close. (b) To hold stitches for cables, use U-shaped holder with points at both ends. Slip specified stitches onto holder and place holder in back or front of work as directed.

Sewing sweater seams

Place pieces right side up and parallel to one another along seam to be sewed. Align pieces. With same yarn in which sweater was worked and yarn or tapestry needle, sew as follows: Take one small running stitch in edge of right piece; take one par-allel running stitch in edge of left piece. Beginning at end of first stitch, take one small running stitch in edge of right piece; take one small parallel running stitch in edge of left piece. Repeat until seam is completed.

Other Abbreviations

begin = beg
contrasting color = cc
double-pointed (needles) = dp
main color = mc
remaining = rem
stitch = st
together = tog

Crochet

General Information

Depending on the yarn and the size of the hook, you can crochet a variety of items from the finest, most delicate lace doily to a heavy and handsome wall hanging. All crochet work is based on the principle of pulling yarn through loops with a hook; chain stitch, which begins any crochet work, is the simplest form of yarn-through-loop.

Practice each of the stitches to be sure you can crochet a few rows evenly before you begin work on a crochet project. Always start your work with a foundation chain. When you count chains to start a row of stitches, do not count the loop on the hook as one chain.

When you insert the hook into the stitches, be sure it is inserted under the top two threads of the stitch. To make second and subsequent rows, end the previous row by making as many chain stitches as instructions indicate; then turn and, skipping the chain stitches, insert hook into first stitch of previous row and continue working as before.

Stitches and terms

Crochet instructions are written using many abbreviations. The abbreviations are shown in parentheses after the stitch or term.

Chain (ch) (Fig. 1)

Make a slip knot and place it over the hook. Hold yarn in left hand as shown and place hook under yarn, then over yarn to form a loop over hook. Pull yarn through slip-knot loop. You now have a new loop on hook; 1 chain is made.

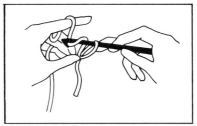

FIG. 1
CHAIN

Single crochet (sc) (Fig. 2)

Insert the hook in the 2nd chain from the hook (Fig. 2A). Place hook under then over yarn as shown (this is called yarn over). Pull yarn through the loop on hook; now there are 2 loops on hook. Yarn over again (Fig. 2B) and pull yarn through both loops. Now there is 1 loop on hook; 1 sc is made (Fig. 2C). Continue working in this manner in each ch. To turn, ch 1.

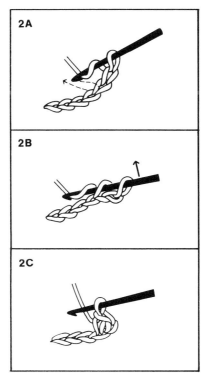

FIG. 2
SINGLE CROCHET

Double crochet (dc) (Fig. 3)

Yarn over. Insert hook into 4th chain from hook (Fig. 3A). Yarn over <u>again</u> and pull yarn through the 4th chain. Now there are 3 loops on hook. Yarn over and pull yarn through 1st 2 loops on hook (Fig. 3B). Now there are 2 loops on hook. Yarn over and pull yarn through these 2 loops (Fig. 3C). Now there is 1 loop on hook; 1 dc is made. Continue working in this manner in each ch. To turn, ch 3.

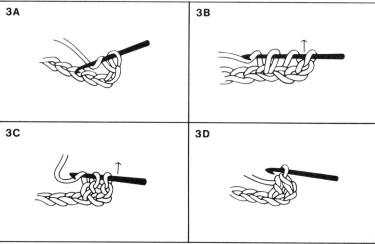

FIG. 3
DOUBLE CROCHET

Half double crochet (hdc) (Fig. 4)

Yarn over. Insert hook into 3rd chain from hook (Fig. 4A). Yarn over <u>again</u> and pull yarn through the 3rd chain. Now there are 3 loops on hook. Yarn over and pull yarn through all 3 loops on hook (Fig. 4B). Now there is 1 loop on hook; 1 hdc is made (Fig. 4C). Continue working in this manner in each ch. To turn, ch 2. <u>Increasing hdc:</u> Work 2 hdc into 1 st. <u>Decreasing hdc</u> (at beginning of row): Skip 1st stitch and work 1st hdc into 2nd stitch of previous row.

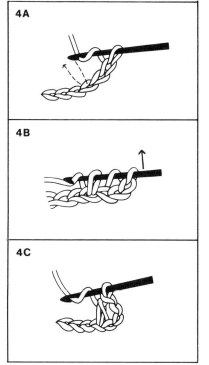

FIG. 4
HALF DOUBLE CROCHET

Slip stitch (sl st) (Fig. 5)

Insert hook in 2nd chain from hook. Yarn over and pull yarn through both the chain and the loop on the hook. Now there is 1 loop on hook; 1 sl st is made. Continue working in this manner in each ch. To turn, ch 1. Always use sl st for joining.

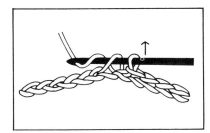

FIG. 5
SLIP STITCH

Gauge

Instructions frequently specify how many stitches to the inch are required to complete the project successfully. Always test gauge before beginning a project. To test your gauge, ch 20-30, using hook size and yarn specified in instructions. Work 3'' in stitch used for greatest proportion of item. Smooth out swatch, pin down and measure. If you have more stitches and rows to the inch than specified, use a larger hook. If you have fewer, use a smaller hook. If necessary, crochet new swatches with larger or smaller hooks until the gauge is correct.

Yarn over (yo)

The action of looping the yarn over hook.

Attach

To attach a new skein or ball of same or different color, overlap old and new threads, working 1 stitch with double thread. Drop old thread and continue working with new. When piece is completed, weave in all tails.

Fasten off

Cut the yarn, leaving a 3''-4'' tail. Pull the tail through the last loop on the hook. Weave in tail.

Weave in

Thread the yarn tail into a tapestry or other large-eyed needle; then weave it back over and under the strands of a few stitches. Always weave yarn into same-color stitches. Trim end close to work.

Other abbreviations

begin = beg
increase = inc
decrease = dec
space(s) = sp(s)
stitch(es) = st(s)
round(s) = rnd(s)
together = tog
main color = mc
contrasting color = cc
* * = do what is in asterisks the number of times specified after 2nd asterisk

Embroidery

General Information

Embroidery is a popular art throughout the world partly because with so few materials, so much can be done. All you need is needle and thread, fabric and scissors. Then choose your design and your stitches and you're ready to go! Use embroidery as an art form in and of itself or embellish garments or household items with embroidery designs. Just about anything made from fabric can be adorned with embroidery.

Needles

When you purchase your materials, be sure to choose a needle that will make a hole of just the right size—large enough for thread to go through without tearing fabric fibers, but not so large that the hole will show after stitching. Needles are sized 1-12, with 12 as the smallest.

Hoop and frame

Use a hoop or frame to hold your fabric taut so you will have a flat surface on which to work. To use a screw-type hoop (the best kind), place the smaller circle on a flat surface; place the fabric with design over it; place the larger circle on top of fabric and push down over smaller circle, pulling fabric so it becomes taut. Tighten screw.

Frames (stretchers) can be purchased, or you can make one with four strips of wood. Use tacks to attach fabric. When working, set one side of the frame on your lap and the other on a table.

Stitches

Satin stitch (Fig. 1)

Straight stitches made very close together but not overlapping (Fig. 1A). Needle will always come up on one side and go down on the other side of the area you are working. When working slanted satin stitch (Fig. 1B), begin stitching in center of design (arrow) to keep stitches uniform.

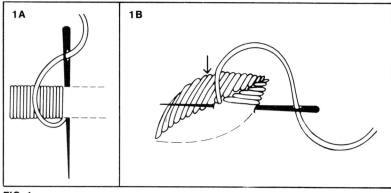

FIG. 1
SATIN STITCH

Long and short stitch (Fig. 2)

Same as satin stitch except stitches are alternately long and short. When you work a 2nd row, put long stitches opposite short stitches of 1st row.

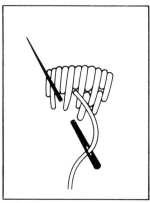

FIG. 2
LONG AND SHORT STITCH

Chain stitch (Fig. 3)

Each chain is a loop of thread left after you take a stitch in the fabric. Size of stitch you take will determine size and uniformity of loops.

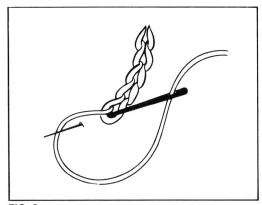

**FIG. 3
CHAIN STITCH**

Lazy daisy (Fig. 4)

Follow chain stitch technique (Fig. 4A); then bring needle down again on opposite (outer) side of loop, taking small stitch to fasten loop to fabric (Fig. 4B). Petals of daisy should all begin at a central point.

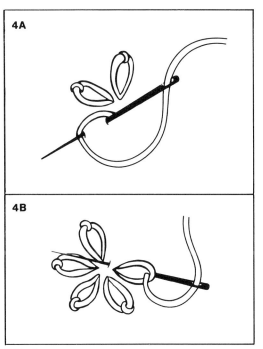

**FIG. 4
LAZY DAISY**

Stem stitch (Fig. 5)

Take stitches on slight diagonal to imaginary line of work. Work from left to right.

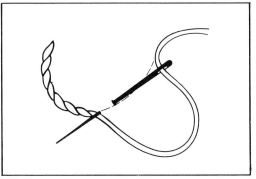

**FIG. 5
STEM STITCH**

French knot (Fig. 6)

Bring needle up at desired position of knot. Hold thread taut and wrap it around needle 1-3 times (Fig. 6A), depending on how large you want knot to be. Still holding thread taut, bring needle down next to where it came up (Fig. 6B), but not in same place or you will lose knot.

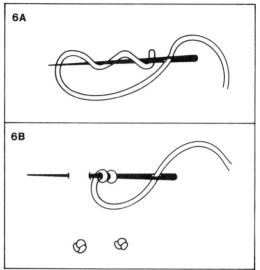

FIG. 6
FRENCH KNOT

Cross-stitch (Fig. 7)

Bring needle up at 1, down at 2, up at 3, down at 4 and so forth to make a row of half cross-stitches. Then work the same row in the opposite direction, bringing needle up at 5, down at 6, up at 7 and so forth.

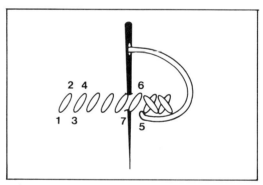

FIG. 7
CROSS-STITCH

Buttonhole (blanket) stitch (Fig. 8)

Bring needle up at 1, down at 2 and up at 3, keeping thread under needle as shown in Fig. 8A. Point 3 then becomes 1 for the next stitch. Work stitches far apart (Fig. 8A) or close together (Fig. 8B).

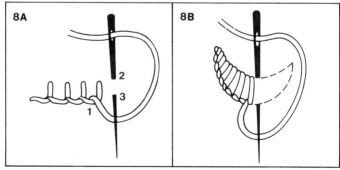

FIG. 8
BUTTONHOLE (BLANKET) STITCH

Couching stitch (Fig. 9)

Lay 1 thread (take a large stitch) on fabric in desired position. With 2nd thread of same or different color, take small stitches over 1st thread at even intervals.

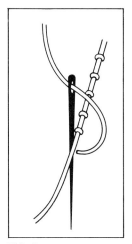

**FIG. 9
COUCHING STITCH**

Cretan feather stitch (Fig. 10)

Overlap a series of short stitches on a diagonal. To fill an area, work rows side by side.

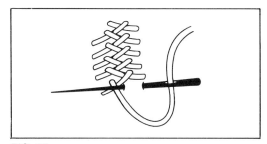

**FIG. 10
CRETAN FEATHER STITCH**

Running stitch (Fig. 11)

Take a series of short straight stitches in a straight line. The spaces between the stitches should be approximately the same size as the stitches themselves.

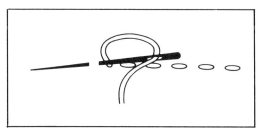

FIG. 11

Split stitch (Fig. 12)

Bring needle down as if to make a running stitch (Fig. 12A), then up in the center of the stitch between the strands of thread (Fig. 12B). Continue in this manner, keeping all stitches uniform (Fig. 12C).

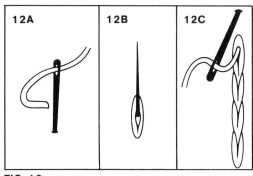

12A **12B** **12C**

Straight stitch (not shown)

A single stitch used as an accent.

FIG. 12

Needlepoint

General Information

Canvas

Needlepoint canvas is purchased according to the number of mesh (holes) per inch. Double-thread canvas is called Penelope; single-thread canvas is called mono. Quickpoint is almost always done on 5 mesh canvas. Each square of the grids in our needlepoint patterns represents a square on your canvas. Be sure to purchase no less, and often more, than the specified amount of canvas. With masking tape, tape the edges of the canvas before beginning so they will not fray yarns.

Designs on a grid

Fold the canvas in fourths, and mark the center lines by pulling a pencil down them. If desired, with light pencil mark the center lines of the printed design as well. Begin stitching in the middle of the canvas so your finished work will be symmetrical. When counting, count the threads and not the holes since each stitch is made over a thread.

Tracing onto canvas

Always use a permanent needlework marker for tracing; it should not run during blocking. Test with water to be sure marks do not run before beginning tracing. Fold the canvas in fourths and mark the center lines by pulling a pencil down them. With paper and fine-line marker, draw the full-size design, then place the marked canvas over the design and draw design on canvas with permanent marker.

Stitching

Use a blunt tapestry needle; the point of other types of needles will split the wool. To begin, go down (from right to wrong side of canvas) a few stitches away from where you are beginning. Come up at your 1st stitch, then as you proceed work over 1st piece of yarn on wrong side, cutting it off on right side when it is securely locked in. To end off, weave needle and yarn in and out of backs of stitches; never end off a dark color into light-color stitches as the dark might show through. To begin the next strand and all other strands, weave in and out through backs of stitches as you did to end off.

Blocking

Finished needlepoint pieces are almost always out of shape from handling and from the action of the yarn. Pieces that will be stretched over a backing do not need to be blocked; they will regain their correct conformation when stretched. Rugs and pieces that will be mounted as wall hangings must be blocked.

You need

- Needlepoint piece
- Wool-cleaning soap or soap flakes
- Piece of wood larger than needlepoint
- Rustproof tacks or nails
- Hammer
- Cardboard tube (optional)

To block

1. Determine correct finished size of needlepoint.

2. Rinse needlepoint in clear lukewarm water, or if it is soiled, in soapy lukewarm water. If desired, have needlepoint dry cleaned.

3. Rinse needlepoint in clear water and tack or nail to wood, pulling to measured finished size.

4. Let dry completely (at least a few days) away from direct heat. Weight the corners to prevent curling. Mount it immediately or roll it right-side out around a tube for storage.

Stitches

Continental (Fig. 1)

Bring needle up at 1, down at 2, up at 3 and so forth, working right to left. At end of row, turn canvas upside down and continue, still working right to left. Turn canvas after each row and always work right to left.

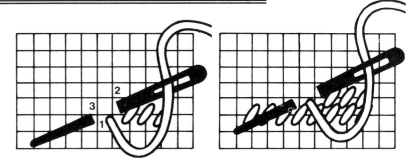

Cross-stitch (Fig. 2)

With Penelope (double-thread) canvas, bring needle up at 1, down at 2, up at 3, down at 4 and so forth to make a row of half cross-stitches. Then work the same row in the opposite direction, bringing needle up at 5, down at 6, up at 7 and so forth.

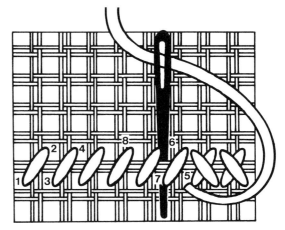

Upright Gobelin (Fig. 3)

This stitch crosses completely over 3 mesh and is straight rather than slanted. Bring needle up at 1, down at 2, up at 3, down at 4 and so forth. Canvas does not need to be turned to work 2nd and subsequent rows.

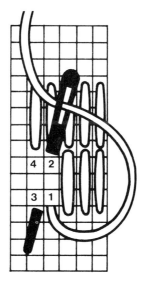

Photography credits

Dust jacket: Larry Dale Gordon. Pages **10-11**: Rick Mitchell; **13-14**, **16**, **18-19**: Robert Keeling; **20-21**: Richard Foster; **25**: Robert Keeling; **28-31**: Tutt Esquerre; **32-33**: Tets Itahara; **35-37**: Tom Benda; **38**: Suzanne Seed; **41-42**: Kazu; **44-45**: Peter Levy; **47**: Robert Keeling; **49-51**: Tutt Esquerre; **52-55**, **57**: Richard Foster; **58-59**: Jerry Salvati; **62-63**: Tutt Esquerre; **65**: Michael Raab; **66**: Richard Tomlinson; **69**, **72-74**: Tets Itahara; **75-77**: Robert Keeling; **78-81**: Tom Benda; **82-83**: Michael Raab; **86-90**: Dennis Menarchy; **91,93**: Frances McLaughlin-Gill; **96-104**: Larry Dale Gordon; **105**: Jerry Salvati; **106-109**: Jerry Brody; **110-112**: Robert Keeling; **114**: Tutt Esquerre; **116-119**: Robert Keeling; **122-123**: Tutt Esquerre; **125**: Steinbicker/ Houghton; **127**: Tets Itahara; **128-130**: Robert Keeling; **132**: Norman Mosallem; **135-136**: Larry Dale Gordon; **138**: Carmen Schiavone; **143**: Tutt Esquerre; **146**: Victor Skrebneski; **149**: Richard Foster; **150**: Tutt Esquerre; **152-153**: Robert Keeling; **155**: Tets Itahara; **158**: Barbara Bordnick; **160**, **162**: Robert Keeling; **164-167**: Taber Chadwick; **168**: Dennis Menarchy; **172-175**: Tutt Esquerre

Design credits

Dust jacket: Marc Belenchia. Pages **10-12**: Nina Ward; **13-15**: Deborah Webster; **16-17**: Deborah Webster; **18-19**: Made by John Widmer; **20-24**: ReShard Frémantle; **25-27**: Caroline Kriz; **28-31**: Janice Arnow; **32-34**: Virginia Bath; **35-37**: Stan Smetkowski; **38-40**: Suzanne Seed; **41-43**: Natasha Mayers; **44-45**: William Accorsi; **46-48**: Harold Cook; **49-51**: Southern Highland Handicraft Guild; **52-55**: Monique Kilcher; **56-57**: Jim Barlow; **58-61**: Virginia Bath; **62-63**: Barbara Standish; **64-65**: Susan Ross for Coats and Clark; **66-67**: Joan Gilbert; **68-71**: Barbara Standish; **72-74**: Grace Jakubs; **75-77**: Valborg Linn; **78-81**: Down to Earth and The Greenhouse; **82-85**: Stephanie Mallis; **86-90**: Charleen Kinser and M. F. White; **91-95**: Carol Hart; **96-97**: Charleen Kinser; **98-104**: Fran Paulson; **105**: Barbara Hanna; **106-109**: Kendix; **110-112**: Chicago Historical Society; **113-115**: Eunice Svinicki; **116-121**: Deborah Webster (tray and stand); Rodica Prato (tile); **122-123**: Virginia Bath; **124-126**: Will and Eileen Richardson; **127**: Becky Bisioulis; **128**: Deborah Webster and Fritzie Pantoga; **132-134**: Ruth Rohn; **135-137**: Marc Belenchia; **138-139**: Martha Kazelunas for Bucilla; **140-142**: Kathleen Holmes; **143-145**: Virginia Bath; **146-147**: Sherl Nero; **148-149**: Rita Di Cesare Saunders; **150-151**: Norala Arts; **152-154**: Robert Chodzinski; **155-157**: Judy Olesch; **158-159**: Ruth Rohn for Reynolds Yarns; **160-163**: John Widmer (hanging lamp); Barbara Standish and David Warren (basket lamp); **164-167**: Charleen Kinser; **168-171**: Charleen Kinser; **172-175**: Caroline Kriz